C00019649O

ANCIENT MAGIC

PHILIP MATYSZAK

ANCIENT MAGIC

✴

A PRACTITIONER'S GUIDE
TO THE SUPERNATURAL
IN GREECE AND ROME

Frontispiece: Feeding the sacred snakes at
the Temple of Asclepius on the island of Cos.

First published in the United Kingdom in 2019
by Thames & Hudson Ltd, 181A High Holborn,
London WC1V 7QX

Ancient Magic © 2019 Thames & Hudson Ltd, London
Text © 2019 Philip Matyszak

British Library Cataloguing-in-Publication Data
A catalogue record for this book is available from the British Library

ISBN 978-0-500-05207-5

Printed in China by Shanghai Offset Printing Products Limited

To find out about all our publications, please visit
www.thamesandhudson.com. There you can subscribe
to our e-newsletter, browse or download our current catalogue,
and buy any titles that are in print.

CONTENTS

�֯

�֯

Mercury [Hermes] Trismegistus, 'Born of great Jupiter, with that
force of inspired divine mind and high awareness of heaven'.

DISCOVERING ANCIENT MAGIC

To study ancient magic, start by forgetting about the 'supernatural'. In the ancient world, there was no such thing. This is not because nothing was magical in that world, but because everything was. The ancient world was numinous, which means 'infused with divine power'. Nature was packed with magic. Flowers turned magically into fruit, and caterpillars into butterflies. Magic filled clouds with energy enough to destroy a house with one well-aimed thunderbolt. The natural *was* supernatural, and to the Greeks and Romans, 'magic' was the use of natural forces to bring about a desired result.

You could do magic by planting an acorn and creating an oak tree, harnessing the powers of water and time. When you think about it, bringing into being a magnificent oak tree (complete with its own dryad) is certainly a feat of which any wizard should be proud.

Of course, performing some magic required complicated rituals or formulas. Success was not guaranteed – but then you can say the same thing about baking bread. After all, the ancients did not know what yeast was, but they understood how to make a delicious loaf. Casting a spell or baking a bun involved the same fundamental principles. You assembled a list of ingredients, mixed them under the right conditions, then waited hopefully while materials you vaguely understood interacted in ways that you didn't understand at all. Whether you were invoking *Lactobacillus sanfranciscensis* or the chthonic spirit of Hermes Trismegistus (Thrice-Great) was immaterial; both were magical creatures.

The world was overpopulated with such creatures. Every garden probably had at least a dozen. Each tree had a dryad, every pool its own nymph, and Nereids frolicked in the waves at the beach. And that's before we count the magical creatures that today we regard as everyday animals – weasels, woodpeckers and wolves among them. Every natural place had its own *genius loci*, a natural force that lent its spirit to the atmosphere of that place. To perform magic, the trick was to be able to work with such forces – forces that were invisible and mysterious, but very real.

So forgetting about the 'supernatural' is a start. Yet to understand magic in the ancient world, we have to forget about so much more. In the modern world – and especially in the West – religion has long claimed a monopoly on dealings with unseen powers and forces. There was no such monopoly in antiquity. Religion, usually state-sponsored and a civic duty, kept the peace between men and gods, but it was mythology that humanized those gods, and explained how the universe had come into being and how it functioned. Then there was magic, used by ordinary people to interact directly with the unseen.

This is a world where gods, like humans, were creatures of space and time; where humans might not just talk to spirits and deities,

Nereid riding a *ketos* (sea monster).

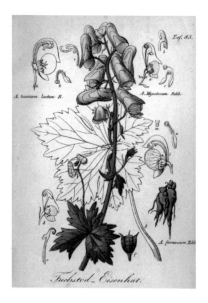

Wolfsbane. It doesn't just kill wolves...

but even themselves become divine. In short, imagine a world where anything is possible. This was the magical world of antiquity.

This view of the world might not be as outlandish as it at first appears. Current research into chaos theory and quantum effects have shown that not everything is predictable or knowable; 'reality' may be completely different from what we imagine it to be. This book explores one of these alternative realities; a reality in which it is possible to make a love potion, craft a curse or talk to the dead. It will show you how to identify and expel evil spirits, and ward off werewolves and vampires.

However, we would also like to stress that knowing *how* to do something does not mean that you *should* do it. The Romans killed anyone found with wolfsbane growing in their garden, and accepted no excuses, because it is child's play to make a deadly poison from this unassuming plant. The ancients were often quick to judge – and punish – anyone they suspected of using illicit magic, not because they did not understand it, or because they feared 'the supernatural', but because some activities are basically antisocial, or downright dangerous, and need to be firmly discouraged.

This remains true today. It is not illegal to call yourself a witch or a wizard in most Western societies. Nevertheless, some elements of the craft remain highly illegal, and dangerous to the practitioner and everyone around them. For example, while this book will tell you how the ancients summoned demons and the other spirits of the Underworld, it is strongly recommended that readers do not try such a ritual at home. At best, the experiment will fail, wasting both your time and several bucketloads of sheep's blood. At worst – you might succeed.

Νεϰρομαντεία
TALKING TO THE DEAD

> To ask questions of a corpse: Take a leaf of flax, and
> on it write these twelve letters: AZEL BALEMACH*
>
> The ink must be made from red ochre, juice of fresh
> wormwood [*Artemisia absinthium*], burnt myrrh,
> evergreen needles and flax. Write as instructed and
> put it in the [corpse's] mouth.[1]

It is proverbial that anyone can talk to the dead if they really want
to. The difficult part is getting the dead to talk back. Accomplishing
that requires specialist skills, or the assistance of someone who has
them – someone who can reach through the veil between the living
and the dead, and draw the spirits of the departed back to this world.
That someone is a necromancer.

Necromancy was once a common form of divination in the ancient
world, and if done in the right way by the right people it was not
particularly disreputable. In fact, we shall examine in detail the
techniques for talking with the dead that were used by none other
than the legendary hero Odysseus. The techniques of the art were
established by the Babylonians and Persians (Persian necromancers
were called 'Magi' or 'Necyomanteis'), and were enthusiastically
adopted by the Greeks and Romans.

Today, necromancy is considered a dark craft, not least because
it is strictly forbidden by the Bible: 'There shall not be found among

* Use small letters – even a large flax leaf is only 4 cm (1½ in.) long.

you anyone who calls up the dead. For whoever does these things is detestable to the Lord'.[2] Of course, this did not stop King Saul from asking the Witch of Endor to summon the spirit of the prophet Samuel, but Saul did get a good telling off from Samuel for doing so.[3] The Biblical injunction against the practice means that necromancy is counted today as one of the black arts – especially the kind of necromancy allegedly perpetrated by some Roman aristocrats, which involved the ritual slaughter of young boys: 'You had begun your esoteric and sacrilegious sacrifices, being accustomed to calling up the spirits of the underworld and appeasing them with the intestines of murdered boys.'[4]

Talking to the dead is not easy, and even 'respectable' rites become more difficult as the deceased becomes more distant in space and time; necromancy is easiest when the corpse is freshly dead and right in front of the practitioner. Leave it too long and there are very practical reasons why you cannot talk to the spirits of the dead at all – mostly because they have stopped being dead.

Thanatos (Death) and Hypnos (Sleep) carry away the Greek hero Sarpedon, while the slain warrior's spirit flies away between them.

Samuel's ghost informs King Saul that he will soon be joining him.

The Necromantic Witch of Endor

When Saul, king of the Israelites wanted to know what to do about the Philistines, diviners and prophets proved useless. In desperation, Saul asked a famed witch to raise the spirit of the prophet Samuel.

Then the woman said, 'Whom shall I bring up for you?' And he said, 'Bring me up Samuel.' When the woman saw Samuel, she cried out with a loud voice, she spoke to Saul, saying, 'Why have you deceived me? For you are Saul!'

And the king said to her, 'Be not be afraid. What did you see?'

And the woman said to Saul, 'I saw gods ascending out of the earth.'

So he said to her, 'What is his form?' And she said, 'An old man is coming up, and he is covered with a mantle.' And Saul perceived that it was Samuel, and he stooped with his face to the earth and bowed himself down.[5]

A very annoyed Samuel informed Saul that he and his army would perish the very next day – and so it came to pass.

To understand why this is so, we must answer a fundamental question – who are the dead? The answer can't be as simple as 'people who are not alive'. While we have a pretty good idea of what is involved in being alive, there is very little agreement on what happens after that. Are the dead immaterial souls transported to a realm far from our own, matrixes of energy trapped by the place and circumstances of their death, or peaceful mounds of mouldering earth? Or any and all of the above? Until this has been established, no necromancer can get very far. It's hard to have a conversation if you don't know who – or what – you are talking to.

From the Greek and Roman point of view, being dead is actually the default condition of humanity. The spirits of the dead are worth talking to because they exist outside of time; to them, the future is as clear as the past, making spirits a useful contact for those seeking to know how their own lives on earth will turn out. Humans, essentially, are like the gods – immortal and indestructible. The body might die (and it frequently does), but the spirit it contains cannot be destroyed. At any given time, most of the human race dwells among the shadows of the Underworld. That's why the god Hades, ruler of the Underworld, has the dread name of Pluto – it means 'the Lord of Many'. Since the human spirit is indestructible, the very worst that even the gods can do to a human is make life – using the term 'life' rather loosely – as miserable as possible. That's where the mythical stories of the torture of Sisyphus and Tantalus come from. For cheating the gods Sisyphus is doomed to roll a stone up a hill for eternity; each time he nears the top, the stone rolls down again. Tantalus is punished for serving the gods a cannibalistic meal by being, well, tantalized by food and drink forever kept just beyond his reach.

However, such cases are exceptional. For most of humanity, the punishment for misbehaviour while alive is having plenty of time to regret it while dead. There was considerable disagreement among ancient philosophers about how sentient the spirits of the dead were,

An Underworld idyll, with Charon paddling over the Styx, Hades and
Persephone in the background, and Cerberus lazing in the corner.

but the consensus was that compared to the world of the living, the
Underworld was a grey, sterile place. It had to be. Ancient philoso-
phy teaches that life on this earth is lived at an unsustainable pitch.
Humans are wrenched by emotion, torn by conflicting urges and
desires, and wracked by hungers and pains both physical and mental.
An eternity of this would drive any being to insanity. So death takes
them into the Underworld – that cool, passionless place over the
River Styx. Outside of time, the pent-up energies and overwrought

feelings of the living soul slowly drain away, leaving the spirit with a clear idea of what went right or wrong in their past life, and how to do better next time.

For there is a next time. After a period of reflection, a spirit feels itself drawn towards one end of the Underworld, where flows the little stream called Lethe. Nearby is a cavern, and within are the descriptions of lives yet to be. These descriptions are called 'lots' and when someone talks about his or her 'lot in life' this is the one they mean. You decide whether to have a short life filled with pain and spiritual development or a meaningless life as a millionaire playboy, and choose your lot accordingly. Then you drink the waters of Lethe, which bring instant forgetfulness. Thereafter you are reborn into the world to live out your chosen destiny:

> The river Lethe flowed quietly through these tranquil
> groves. Through the trees flitted an uncountable multitude.
> Unable to understand, Aeneas asked what it was that
> he saw. The [spirit of his father] Anchises said,
>   'They are souls due reincarnation. Here they crowd the
> river Lethe to drink a deep draught of oblivion, so that
> the waters may wash away their troubles. Cleansed of their
> cares, they return to the world above.'[6]

Of course, once a person is thus reborn, that spirit is out of the reach of necromancy. There is no use in discovering the spirit of Cleopatra if she is currently Doris Smith of Fishgate. That spirit now remembers nothing of her past or future and anyway, by definition, necromancy does not work on the living. Also out of contact are those spirits who have reached the Elysian Fields and evolved to the next level of humanity, forever beyond our reach.

Even narrowing the field to spirits still available, the necromancer must choose a subject carefully. Asking the spirit of an Athenian peasant about the future of Britain is about as productive as asking a toddler about the history of Akkadia. Nor is choosing a particular subject a straightforward process. Calling up the dead is one thing – summoning a specific member of that community is much, much harder.

ODYSSEUS AND TIRESIAS

The following is a summoning of the dead as told by the practitioner of that necromantic act. It is found in Homer's *Odyssey*.[7] (We leave it to the reader to decide how accurately the conjuration is performed. It is important to note that modern scholars feel that some lines are later additions.) Given the perilous journey that lay ahead of him, the hero Odysseus was understandably keen for some suggestions about how best to avoid these dangers. Odysseus was instructed in the necromantic rites by the witch Circe, better remembered for her shape-shifting ability, particularly as applied to his crew (see pp. 63–66). Odysseus hoped to speak to a certain Tiresias, because even in life Tiresias, though blind, was famed for being able to see into the future. Death could only have enhanced that power.

We beached the ship, and taking the sheep with us,
we went along the beach until we reached the site [by
observing the signs] that Circe had described....I drew my
sword and dug a trench a cubit [a length from the elbow
to the middle fingertip] wide and a cubit deep. To the dead
I made an offering of drink, first milk and honey, then of
wine, and then water.
    I sprinkled white barley meal over it all. Then I addressed
the wandering souls. I promised that on returning to Ithaca
I would sacrifice to them the best barren heifer in my herds,

and I would light a sacrificial pyre laden with bounty.
To Tiresias in particular, I pledged a black sheep, the best
of my flock. When the invocation was complete, I slit the
throats of the sheep, so that the blood ran into the trench.

Then the ghosts came flocking from the Underworld...
they came from all directions and swirled about the trench,
while their strange shrieks made me go pale with fear.
At their approach I told my men to quickly skin the sheep,
and burn them as an offering to Hades and Persephone.
Then I drew my sword to keep the spirits of the dead away
from the blood until Tiresias had answered my questions.

This summoning is notable for three factors. First, it seems that a summoning could not be performed just anywhere. It worked best at places where the veil between the worlds of the living and the dead was most thin. A recent battlefield was one such – temporary – location. We will examine some alternative choices later (see pp. 26–33).

Secondly, we see the importance of blood, here paired with white barley – probably the flour known to the ancients as *mola* that was traditionally used in sacrificial rites (which is the reason that modern victims are sometimes described as 'immolated'). The use of blood seems to have been very common in classical necromancy, because the ancients recognized that blood was the power that gave life. Therefore, making blood available to the dead gave them temporary life, something which they craved, as we can see from the rapid approach of a multitude of uninvited spirits. Blood was apparently also needed to permit the actual communication: Odysseus was careful to keep the other spirits away from the blood offering, with the exception of his comrade Elpenor, who was still unburied. Being therefore trapped between existences, Elpenor could converse without first tasting the blood.

Lost spirits swirl in the background as Odysseus consults Tiresias.

Thirdly, the arrival of such a mass of spirits at the conjuration shows that Odysseus had little control over who answered his summons. Some came because they had a personal connection to the hero – but many more were drawn simply by the lure of blood. 'Brides and bachelors, old men worn by their labours, and young men killed in battle, their armour still splattered with gore'; all these Odysseus held at bay with the iron of his sword held over the well of blood. After Tiresias had delivered his prophecy, Odysseus asked him how he could speak to one of the spirits nearby:

But now I need you to tell me truly – my poor mother's spirit sits close nearby; right beside the blood. She says not a word, and though I am her own son she does not remember me. Tell me, great one, how I can get her to recognize me?' 'That I can tell you easily' he [Tiresias] replied. 'Let any spirit drink the blood, and that spirit will talk to you in a sensible fashion. Keep them from the blood and they will lose interest and wander off.' Then, having spoken his prophesy, the spirit of Tiresias returned to the kingdom of Hades. I remained sitting in place until my mother came and tasted the blood. Then at once she recognized me and spoke fondly to me.'....

There seemed no way to embrace her spirit. Three times I tried to hold her in my arms, but each time she flitted away like the phantom she was. Deeply hurt, I asked 'Mother, why do you avoid my embrace? If we could share a hug, we could also share our sorrows, even in the house of Hades. Does Persephone want to add to my grief by mocking me in this way?'

She answered, 'My son, this is not the work of Persephone, but the nature of the dead. When life has left the body the sinews no longer knit flesh and bone together. These are gone in the consuming fire as the spirit flies off as though into a dream...'.

Thereafter, while the blood retained its potency, Odysseus talked long with many of the 'wives and daughters of heroes', though for some reason he seems to have talked only with the womenfolk, and is careful not to tell his audience what he learned. Some secrets are not for sharing.

A WOMAN REANIMATES HER DEAD SON

This is a 'straightforward' necromantic ritual described in a text called the *Aethiopica* of Heliodorus, a Greek writer of the 3rd or 4th century AD. The woman is known only as 'the witch of Bessa', and as it happened, the ritual led directly to her death. However, our interest here is in the ritual itself and how closely it follows that of Odysseus, though the witch had an easier job, having the recently deceased corpse right at hand.

Thinking that she now had time to work undisturbed where no one could see her, the old woman first dug a trench. She made a fire on each side, and laid her son's body between them. Then she took an earthen pot from the three-legged stool which stood nearby, and poured honey into the trench. A second pot was poured, this time of milk, and from a third pot, a libation of wine.

Then she tossed into the trench a doll made from dough. This was in the shape of a man. It had been partly baked in the fire and was garlanded with laurel and fennel. Then she took up a sword...and as though in a Bacchic frenzy she chanted a series of outlandish prayers to the moon. Then she sliced her arm so that the blood fell onto a branch of laurel, which she used to sprinkle blood upon the fire.[8]

This animated her son, but the information he gave his grieving mother made her so distraught that the witch stumbled and impaled herself on an upright spear which was nearby, and she died soon after – exactly as her reanimated son had prophesied.

REVIVING A CORPSE

This text comes from Lucan's *Pharsalia*, a deliberately over-the-top and sensationalist text about the civil war that ended the Roman Republic. It is named after the climactic battle between Caesar and Pompey at Pharsalus in Greece. Lucan's witch, an expert at necromancy, is about as hair-raising a character as it is possible to meet. She was also something of an anomaly – most witches were wise enough not to test their skills in communication with the dead, which had clearly driven this practitioner raving mad:

> Eschewing the criminal rites and malpractices of
> Thessalian witches as not wicked enough, Erichtho had
> turned her loathsome skills to rites previously unknown.
> Neither the gods nor the fact that she was yet alive prevent
> her from knowing the mysteries of subterranean Hades,
> or from hearing the speechless communication of the dead.
> ...if she needs warm blood she unhesitatingly takes it
> gushing from a fresh-cut throat, or slits a womb so that the
> child of the unnatural birth may be placed on the fiery altar
> for a ghoulish feast of still-quivering flesh.

Despite this clearly antisocial behaviour, Erichtho's powers of prophecy interested Sextus Pompeius, the son of Pompey the Great who was understandably anxious to learn the outcome of the struggle between his father and Caesar. Erichtho agreed to meet the enquirer at the site of the recent battle of Pharsalus. The more dead littering a battlefield, the weaker the veil between the living and the dead, which had been repeatedly pierced by the souls of the departed, and the better the chances of finding a decent corpse who could reveal the future. As Erichtho explained to her client:

Erichtho grabs another handful of ingredients while
an appalled young Pompey looks on.

'With so many dead on the field hereabouts, the easiest
thing is to select one of the recently slain. From the mouth
of a body still warm we will get something sensible, rather
than the unintelligible gibberings of some desiccated
corpse.'

The important thing, the witch clarified as she picked through
the heaped bodies, was to choose someone with his lungs intact,
as he would need breath in his reanimated body – not for life, but
for speech.

Finally she selected a corpse, and with a hook inserted through a noose around his neck she dragged it over the rocks and stones to live again at the high rock beside the hollow mountain she had chosen to witness these rites.

She began by wounding the chest anew, and through those openings washed away the clotted gore with fresh blood. Then she added plentiful poisons taken under the light of the moon. There was no lack of froth from the mouths of rabid dogs, and the innards of a lynx and the hump of a foul hyaena....

'I invoke the Furies...the ruler of the world below... and Persephone, and our patron Hecate, who permits me speechless converse with the dead...and by any infant who would have lived were not his head and organs laid on my dedicatory plates, I demand you grant my wish. I ask not for a spirit who has lurked long in the Underworld and is accustomed to its shadows, but for one just descended, with the light still behind him; who still lingers on the brink of the chasm.'

When the spirit appeared, it shrank from re-entering its body, until finally, compelled by the witch's threats, 'it abandoned that last gift of death – that the body should not once more perish.'

Every limb quivered and each sinew strained. Then he arose, not limb by limb, but as though bouncing up from the earth to stand upright all at once. This mouth gaped, and though his eyes were open, he looked not like a man alive, but like a man about to die.

Despite the witch's promise of a clear and unambiguous prophecy, all the corpse could say was that the recently dead had not yet renounced the cares of the living, and the dead partisans on each side were determined to continue their struggle in the Underworld. In the end young Sextus was left as uncertain of his future as before. 'Who will be buried by the Nile, and who shall lie beside the Tiber – that is all this struggle will determine. For yourself, ask not your destiny – Fate will make that clear.'

> Having spoken, the corpse stood sorrowfully, in his silence demanding to die once more. Yet death had done its worst to him already, and could not now claim his life again. Spells and drugs were needed before he could return to death. The witch had prepared a great pyre of wood, and the dead man walked to the lighted fire and laid himself upon it, and there they left him to pass away once more.[9]

This text was not intended as an instruction, but as a lurid horror story designed to raise delicious shivers of fear in the audience. Apart from the extreme difficulty of obtaining some of the ingredients of the life-restoring potion (the full dose takes several pages of text to describe), it apparently took a witch of Erichtho's power to make it all work. Of course, she could have been putting on a show for Sextus, vastly exaggerating the difficulty of the rites. Nevertheless, unlike our modern world, in which many delight in playing with ouija boards and holding seances, the message is clearly that in the ancient world, communication with the dead was best left to professionals.

Erichtho's methods have common ground with the altogether less demented rite performed by Odysseus, including the importance of blood and an appropriate location. The Underworld does not interface evenly with the world of the living, and even the most effective ritual will fail if the Underworld cannot be reached from the place where the rites are being performed. Battlefields are an effective shortcut, but even better is a place where the two worlds naturally intersect.

PORTALS TO THE UNDERWORLD
The Necromanteion

The classical Underworld is a physical place, every bit as real as this world. Spirits pass through it, of course, but living humans can also visit (under exceptional circumstances). Rivers that flow across the land of the living on occasion take a downward plunge and run also through the Underworld. Three such rivers are the appropriately named Acheron ('Joyless River'), Cocytus ('Lamentation') and Pyriphlegethon ('River of Burning Coals'). All three rivers join near the city of Thesprotian Ephyra in Epirus in Greece, and not surprisingly, this is the site of the Necromanteion – the Oracle of the Dead. Such was the fame of the Necromanteion that the 2nd-century AD Roman travel-writer Pausanias believed this to be where Odysseus had performed his famous summoning. Certainly the site was known in the Bronze Age, for several children's graves have been found dating to the 13th century BC, roughly contemporary with Odysseus. However, the Necromanteion came into its own during the Archaic era of 800–480 BC, when the site was regularly visited by pilgrims from all over the Greek world. The Greek historian Herodotus, writing in the 5th century BC, tells the story of one such visitor, an emissary of Periander, ruler of Corinth:

> Periander sent messengers to the Oracle of the Dead on the river Acheron in Thesprotia. A friend had left a deposit of money [with Periander's late wife, Melissa] and he wanted to know where it was. The apparition of Melissa appeared, but said she would tell her husband nothing for he had left her cold and naked. Her funeral clothes had never been burned, so they were of no use to her.
>
> To prove that it was the spirit of Melissa herself, she told the messenger to remind Periander that he had put his

loaves into a cold oven. Periander thus knew that the spirit spoke the truth, for he had indulged in intercourse with her corpse.[10]

After deliberating on this message, the king summoned the female aristocracy of Corinth to a celebration at the temple of Hera. Once they were assembled at the temple, the surprised ladies were stripped of their fine garments, which were then burned in a pit (offerings to the Underworld were traditionally immolated in this way, in a sacrifice called a *holocaust*). The luxurious clothing was received by a satisfied Melissa, who thereafter revealed the location of the missing money.

As the oracle became more famous, a temple was built on the site. Enquirers had to undergo an elaborate set of rituals before meeting the spirits of the departed, and adhere to a 'special diet', which might have included hallucinogenic drugs designed to enhance the experience. Archaeological evidence shows that heavy machinery, similar to that used for stage props today added a degree of fakery to the proceedings. In any case, the commonsensical Romans wanted nothing to do with the place, and they demolished it, along with much of the rest of Epirus, in their invasion of 167 BC.

The site was rediscovered in 1958, and at the time of writing those wishing to commune with the oracle are advised by the Greek Ministry of Culture that the Necromanteion is open between 8 a.m. and 5 p.m. every day, and can be accessed by offering a sacrifice of €8. Compared to – for example – the list of ingredients required to concoct Erichtho's potion, this is a real bargain. Those who want even cheaper access near Halloween should note that on 28 October admission is free.

The Gates of Hades at Hierapolis

The 'priestly city' of Hierapolis, in modern-day Turkey, had a famed Plutonium, one of the rarest types of temple in the classical world. Temples to Pluto were usually raised only at 'mephitic' locations – that is, places where poisonous vapours naturally emerge from the ground. (Confusingly, the name 'mephitic' comes from a different deity, Mephitis, the goddess of noxious gases and cat litter boxes.)

Such noxious mists were believed to have wafted directly from the Underworld, and by some accounts the fumes billowing out of the 'Gates of Hades' were powerful enough to kill birds flying overhead and small animals that ventured too close. When the site was excavated in 1965, the gas was discovered to be mainly carbon dioxide, which dissipates harmlessly in open air but causes asphyxiation in high concentrations.

The Gates of Hades. Getting in is easy...

Opportunistic priests of the goddess Cybele built an enclosure at the site, and set themselves up as an oracle of Pluto for those who would ask questions of the dead. The priests claimed that as they were *castrati*, their goddess granted them immunity to its vapours. (Priests of Cybele were castrated in imitation of Cybele's eunuch spouse, Attis.) The Roman historian Cassius Dio (AD 155–235) visited the site in person:

> I have seen such an opening [to the Underworld] at
> Hierapolis in Asia. I tested it with some birds. Bending
> over the opening, I saw the vapour with my own eyes.
> There is a sort of cistern holding it, and they have built a
> temple over it. It kills all living things except *castrati*. I am
> not offering an explanation for this – this is just what
> I experienced for myself.[11]

Those wanting to share the experience of Cassius Dio will be welcomed, as Hierapolis once again has a lively tourist industry. The Plutonium is open to visitors, but no longer kills them – possibly because numerous earthquakes over the centuries have partly closed this portal.

The goddess Cybele, the Great Mother, in her chariot drawn by lions.

CHAPTER ONE

Lake Avernus

Perhaps the Romans were uninterested in the remote Necromanteion of Greece because they believed that there was a portal to the Underworld closer to home. There was good reason for this belief, because Lake Avernus, in southern Italy, is near the volcanic system of the Phlegraean Fields of Cumae. These 'burning fields', with their cratered ground and smoky plumes, certainly give the impression that the Underworld is almost touching the surface. It is also possible that noxious gases emitted from the lake, which is in fact a volcanic crater, poisoned birds that flew too close. The region was originally Greek-speaking, and the Romans believed the word 'Avernus' was derived from *a-ornis*, meaning 'birdless' – 'a' being a Greek prefix meaning 'without' and *ornis* meaning 'bird'.

> The natives tell the story that all birds that fly over it fall down into the water being killed by the vapours that rise from it, as in the case with all the Plutonia.[12]

The same volcanic activity that created the lake also created a system of tunnels nearby. One of these tunnels is almost a kilometre long, and it was believed that, with the right rituals and the right guide one could follow the tunnel even further, right into the Underworld.

Being on the border between the living and the dead, this location was probably the source of the power of the Cumaean Sibyl – a prophetess whose wisdom was eagerly sought by the Romans from earliest times. Indeed, according to the Roman poet Virgil (70–90 BC), it was here, at the Sibyl's direction, that the Trojan hero Aeneas descended to talk to his father in the most dangerous activity in all the perilous profession of necromancy – the κατάβασις (katabasis), literally a 'journey down' to the kingdom of Hades to talk to the dead in their own domain.

Visiting the Underworld

As the Sibyl of Cumae explained to Aeneas, getting to the Underworld
is easy.

> The entrance to dark Hades stands open,
> All day, and all night.
> But to come back again
> To the sweet air of day
> That is a challenge indeed.[13]

Of all the means of talking to the dead, this is the least advisable.
For a start, a descent through any of the portals to the Underworld
requires the assistance of an unearthly guide if the traveller hopes

Engraving by Gustave Doré showing Aeneas and his guide
preparing to descend to the Underworld.

Orpheus pictured just as Hades reclaims his beloved Eurydice.

to make a return journey. Even if the poisonous effects of the caves can be avoided, the actual entrance to the land of the dead may be hidden from mortal eyes. Enthusiastic explorers of the caverns of Lake Avernus have been unable to retrace the Sibyl's route to the Underworld. Another gateway – used by both Hercules and the divine singer Orpheus – was in the caves of Cape Matapan in Tainaron in southern Greece. Pausanias visited these caves to examine the portal, but left disappointed and disillusioned after searching for the Underworld in vain.

At the cape there is a cave-like temple, with a statue of
Poseidon standing in front. The Greek poets say that from
here Hercules dragged up Cerberus from the Underworld.
But no path leads to the Underworld through the cave, nor
is it easy to believe in gods dwelling beneath the earth.[14]

The Greeks and Romans knew of only a handful of living people
who managed to reach the Underworld and get out again in the
same condition. Even then, the minotaur-slaying Theseus had to be
rescued by Hercules. (Theseus' travel companion did not survive.)
Since all successful journeys were accomplished by the semi-human
offspring of Greek gods, only the most egomaniacal of necromancers
would consider this technique.

GHOSTS

You may by now have decided that there is a much simpler way to
talk to the dead – go to a haunted place and speak to a ghost. After

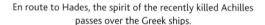

En route to Hades, the spirit of the recently killed Achilles
passes over the Greek ships.

all, this spirit of the dead is pre-summoned, so to speak. All you need is the location, a time, and nerves of steel. However, this means of necromancy is highly unsatisfactory.

It is rather like talking on a cell phone to the captain of a yacht that is sinking in a hurricane. The line of communication is none too good, and the other party knows little of what you want to discuss and cares a great deal less. Rather, now he has got through to someone, he has information of his own that he urgently wants to communicate.

The main difference between the captain of our hypothetical yacht and a ghost is that the ghost is in the room with you, and getting very frustrated. Overall, survivors of the experience do not recommend it.

Pliny's letter to Licinius Sura

The Roman writer and administrator Pliny the Younger (AD 61–113) was open-minded about ghosts (while in a later era, the sceptical playwright George Bernard Shaw was to remark that 'the existence of a liar is easier to believe than the existence of a ghost'). Pliny gave the example of one Curtius Rufus, who, while an impoverished nobody in Africa, met a ghost. Unprompted, the apparition gave Curtius a quick summary of his future, telling him that he would go to Rome and achieve great distinction. Then return to Africa as a provincial governor and there die. Things turned out exactly as predicted, but Pliny himself seems to wonder whether Curtius, by taking the apparition at its word, made his own fortune. When he contracted a minor illness, he convinced himself to death, 'by taking the truth of his future from the experience of his past'.

Pliny goes on to describe a more typical encounter with a ghost uninterested in anything but his own concerns. This ghost was, in stereotypical fashion, an emaciated old man who terrified people by rattling his chains at them in the dead of night. So often and so

The philosopher Athenodorus meets a late-night visitor.

vigorously did the old man do this that he rendered the house he was haunting completely uninhabitable. So far, so standard ghost story. What makes it unusual is the protagonist and what happened next.

Far from being some wild-eyed hysteric, Pliny's protagonist was the grounded philosopher and historian Athenodorus of Canana. Of the generation before Pliny, Athenodorus had been a student of the Stoic astronomer and geographer Posidonius, and was himself tutor to Octavian, the future emperor of Rome. Furthermore, most of his story was independently verified. It began when Athenodorus came to Athens looking for accommodation. He found a notice advertising a house for sale or rent at well below a bargain price.

He became suspicious because the price was so low. Yet once he had been told the story he was far from being scared off. On the contrary, he became all the more eager to rent the house. That evening, he ordered a couch to be set up in the forecourt and told everyone else to go to bed. He had equipped himself with a lamp, a stylus and writing tablets. This was because he wanted his mind to be occupied and not caught up with idle fancies. So closing his mind to the terror of ghosts, ghouls and things that go bump in the night, he focused his imagination upon his work.

The first part of the night passed quietly with him working as usual. Then the clatter and clank of iron became audible. At first Athenodorus simply tried to shut out the noise. He tried to convince himself he was hearing something else, and keeping himself calm, he did not so much as raise his eyes, but instead kept writing. The noise came closer, until it was first at the door, and then in the room with him.

At this point he looked up and saw the ghost, exactly as others had described it. It stood right in front of him, summoning him by beckoning with a finger. Athenodorus gestured to the ghost to wait for a moment, and then went back to his tablets. The ghost came over and rattled his chains right above his head. At this Athenodorus looked up, and seeing that the ghost was beckoning him again, he stood, picked up his lamp and followed it.

The ghost moved slowly, as though weighed down by his chains. Then, as it went around the corner into the courtyard of the house, it abruptly dematerialized. Left alone, Athenodorus piled some grass and leaves to mark the spot where the ghost had vanished.

In the morning, he contacted the city authorities, and advised them to dig up the place he had marked. When this was done, a skeleton was found buried. It was a man, and he had been there for some time, as his bones had mouldered away from the chains which once had fettered his body.

These bones were taken up and buried at public expense. The ghost having been laid to rest with the proper ceremonies, it appeared in the house no more.[15]

Here we appear to have as solid a case of communication with the dead as it is possible to have, given the time and distance from our sources. Pliny himself is far from being a true believer, and the original source was a man of science who tried to make the conditions of the experiment as neutral as possible.

The haunting was known before Athenodorus came to town, so he could not have fabricated this. Nor is it easy to see what the city magistrates might have gained by lying about the existence or state of the body after being sent to dig it up. The problem from the necromancer's point of view is that the encounter yields nothing in terms of information relevant to anyone but the ghost himself. At the very least, the story provides substantial confirmation of the existence of an afterlife, but no one seriously pursuing the path of necromancy should be in any doubt of this anyway.

διάφορες μάγισσες

MAKERS OF MAGIC

Who used magic in antiquity? Does the use of ancient magic require special training, or is one born a witch or wizard? The answer to the first question is 'everybody'. The answer to both parts of the second question is 'no, but it helps'.

Most people today have used ancient magic without even thinking about it. When talking of something bad that might happen, people often remark 'touch wood' while giving the nearest wooden object a quick rap of the knuckles, fearing that they might have 'jinxed' something. This little ritual certainly predates Christianity, and was probably originally an invocation to the woodland god Pan, asking him to break any malignant spell that the speaker had inadvertently cast. Like throwing coins into a fountain (to appease a water deity), and cutting a wedding cake together (for good luck), touching wood is a form of ancient magic.

In the ancient world, this kind of 'everyday magic' was ubiquitous. People routinely used magical talismans to protect them from harm. From birth until adulthood, Roman children wore an amulet called a *bulla* around their necks. This contained whatever protective charms and magical material the family could afford to gather. This custom is not surprising, since in a world without vaccines or antibiotics, infancy was the most dangerous time of life. If they were to survive, children needed all the help they could get – magical or otherwise.

Later in life, the Greeks and Romans routinely checked in with astrologers and other fortune-tellers for advice on everyday decisions.

Marble bust of a Roman boy wearing his *bulla*.

When faced with particularly life-changing dilemmas they would earnestly trek miles to consult a renowned oracle or sibyl (see pp. 171–80).

There were numerous actions that were avoided or performed with magical intent. Superstitious types wouldn't continue down a street if a cat had crossed their path, and before drinking wine, it was usual to splash some from the cup onto the ground as a libation to encourage the benevolence of the gods.

So in one sense, the Greeks and Romans were all magic-users – people who employed forces they didn't understand to obtain results they could not get any other way. The question thus becomes, who practised *serious* magic? (As if using a *bulla* to keep a beloved child alive does not qualify as 'serious'.)

A libation is poured into a *phial*, a sacred bowl used to offer gifts to the gods.

Magic is like most human activities: while some people are gifted with a natural talent, and others are totally helpless, there is no one whose abilities cannot be improved by training and practice. In fact, just being a good student and scrupulously following written instructions could take one far in the magical profession without the need for any innate magical ability. Many an esteemed witch in the ancient world made her name with nothing other than a comprehensive grasp of the natural pharmacopoeia found in the leaves, roots and berries of the local vegetation. Such knowledge was passed down from one witch to the next, regarded with suspicion by the local authorities, and with awe by everyone else. Plenty of magic-users in the ancient world got by with as much magical talent as your corner pharmacist.

Swords and sorcery

A good example of 'practical magic' was the incantation uttered by a blacksmith in the preparation of a sword blade. The incantation worked – but not as the magic-user might have imagined that it did.

The incantation was chanted while the blade was heated in the fire to red-heat before being beaten into shape. The ancients did not know it, but this final heating infused the iron of the blade with carbon from the burning charcoal, thus creating steel. If the blade absorbed too much carbon, then the steel became brittle. Too little, and it remained soft and easily bent (which is a bad thing in a sword).

Therefore, the iron had to be kept in the fire for a precise amount of time – and precise time was hard to measure in a world without clocks. However, if the iron was kept in the fire for exactly the time that it took to chant the incantation, then the chances were good that the blade would absorb just the right amount of carbon to create a good sword and a good reputation for the blacksmith.

Frieze showing a Roman blacksmith at work.

Magic-users needed to learn 'spells', of course, though to the ancients such spells were no more or less supernatural than, for example, the process of preparing willow bark to help rheumatism. Willow bark contains a beta-glucoside called salicin, which has anti-inflammatory properties. The modern synthetic version is marketed as 'Aspirin'. This was another 'spell' that really worked, and theoretically anyone could perform such magic. But without access to the right components and proper execution such 'spells' had a distressing tendency either to fail outright, or to work in unpredictable ways – potentially even more disastrous.

Bungling serious magic can have serious consequences: 'Tullus Hostilius [third king of Rome, incinerated 642 BC] was killed by lightning when he failed to perform the ritual correctly – for they say the words change the significance and outcome of events.'[1] There was also the risk that practising magic would draw upon the practitioner the attention of magical beings, and these beings were not always benevolent. So, while do-it-yourself has always been an option for the general public, serious magic, like serious plumbing and dentistry, is best left to the professionals.

WHAT COULD WITCHES DO?

As we have seen, almost everyone in the ancient world was a magic-user, though some were better at it than others. There were no examinations in the art of witchcraft, and no ceremonies upon achieving that title. One became a magic-user through natural inclination and aptitude. Thereafter, some who had achieved success in the field might take it further and seek out a recognized practitioner in the craft and seek to learn more, and since magic often requires laborious preparation and the gathering of exotic materials, most witches were happy to pass on their experience to anyone prepared

Consulting a witch. This mosaic from the Villa of Cicero in Pompeii
shows a scene from an ancient Greek play.

to do the donkey work. In the *Fasti*, Ovid describes an old woman
surrounded by an attentive circle of girls as she performs a binding
spell, not, apparently, out of any animus against the victim, but to
demonstrate to her audience how it is done.[2]

Perhaps a good analogy is cookery in the modern world. Almost
everyone tries it at some point. Some individuals have discovered
that they can't boil an egg, but others develop an aptitude. Most
stick to routine cookery with a few recipes that they use on special
occasions. Others take things further still and collect recipe books,
and exchange tips and techniques with like-minded colleagues. Some
become journeyman cooks, working in hamburger trucks and fast-
food joints, while others seek out kitchens in top restaurants, travel
far to work under the best chefs, and eventually try to build a reputation of their own. Like chefs, witches were judged by reputation

and results, not qualifications. Also like chefs, some had a wide range of skills and others specialized in a particular aspect of the craft. So what were those aspects?

Herbology

Herbs played a key role in most magical conjurations. Knowing which herbs did what, and the correct way of harvesting them, was a vital part of every witch's education. The following spell for increasing the potency of ingredients when harvested shows how 'everyday' magic and the 'supernatural' (to use modern terms) are inextricably interwoven in the ancient use of these powers. It also shows that in the Greek and Roman mind, magic was generally more effective when it was someone else's. Therefore, 'Greek and Roman' magic borrowed heavily from the Etruscans, the Assyrians and the Egyptians, Scythians and Jews – and sometimes several of these in the same spell. Hence the presence of 'Kronos', a proto-god from Greek myth, and Amun, a senior god from Egypt. Even when a spell was unique to the Greeks or Romans, it was sometimes disguised with a foreign flavour, much as some modern recipes, such as chicken korma, are unknown in their alleged country of origin. This spell, like many in this book, comes from the *Papyri Graecae Magicae*, a collection of Greek spells discovered in Egypt. There were once many other such collections, but the authorities disapproved of them. The emperor Augustus alone ordered the destruction of over 2,000 magical scrolls.

> The Egyptians always obtain their herbs in this manner.
> Firstly the herbalist cleanses himself. Then as he circles the plant three times, he sprinkles it with natron [bi-carbonate of soda] and fumigates it with pine resin.
> Then he burns *kyphi* [Egyptian incense] and pours a libation of milk. As he pulls up the plant he invokes

Hermes rushes to the rescue with a sprig of holy moly
in the 13th-century Codex Medicina Magica.

the name of the power to whom the use of the plant is
dedicated, and calls on that power to make the use more
effective.

This is the invocation:

'Sown by Kronos, conceived by Hera, grown by Ammon
[Amun] and born of Isis, you were watered by Zeus of the
Rains, and nourished by the sun and dew. The dew of the
Gods, the heart of Hermes, the seed of the original Gods in
the eye of the sun and moon, you are the power of Osiris, the

beauty and glory of Ouranos, you embody the soul of Osiris, which is everywhere in joy, you are the spirit of Ammon.

As you have made Osiris exalted, be yourself exalted. Now rise as the sun rises each day. You are as the sun at noon, your roots are from the earth, your powers are from the heart of Hermes, your fibres are the bones of Mnevis [the holy bull of Heliopolis]. Your bloom is the eye of Horus, your seed is the seed of Pan. In bathing you with this resin [smoke] I so honour the gods as I would my own well-being. Be cleansed by prayer and give us power as do Athena and Ares [i.e. wisdom and strength]. I am as Hermes, and I acquire you with Good Fortune at my side, at a propitious hour on a propitious day, that you be effective in all things.'

After this the harvested plant is rolled into a pure linen cloth. Where the roots have been dug up are poured seven seeds of wheat and seven of barley, both mixed with honey.[3]

Witches used herbs for a variety of purposes.

The Papyri Graecae Magicae

When Westerners of the early modern era became interested in ancient Egyptian artefacts, enterprising Egyptians rooted through graves and other ancient sites for materials to sell. Papyrus survives in the dry Egyptian climate, and gradually collectors accumulated scrolls and scraps into small libraries. One such library consisted of spells, incantations and formulas for potions, most dating from the period 100 BC–AD 400. Mostly these spells were notes by professional sorcerers, written to remind themselves of ingredients and formulas. As a result the spells are often cryptic and incomplete. Occasionally they contain deliberate magical booby-traps by way of discouraging their use if they fell into the wrong hands. Anyone contemplating using such spells today should note that the ancient magicians almost certainly would count theirs as 'the wrong hands'.

Medical uses As far as the Greeks and Romans were concerned, medicine – even deadly potions – was on a continuum with magic. 'Neither potent herbs, nor prayer, nor magic spells shall make of you a mother' the poet Ovid tells a woman in his *Fasti*.[4] If a person was cured by herbs administered with a magical incantation, who was to know if it was the magic, the herb or the combination of the two that was effective? Both medicine and spells were hit-and-miss,

A physician prepares a potion in this copy of the *Materia Medica* of Dioscorides. Like many rare ancient texts, this was preserved in Arabic in a folio from Iraq.

The medicinal hare

Pliny the Elder (AD 23–79), a Roman author who died while stationed in the Bay of Naples as a result of the eruption of Vesuvius that buried Pompeii, offers the following statement that illuminates the close relationship between medicine and magic: 'It is the blood of a hare's fœtus that the magicians recommend males to drink [for fertile semen]: while for young girls they prescribe nine pellets of hare's dung to ensure a durable firmness to the breasts.'[5]

sometimes worked and sometimes inexplicably failed or produced adverse results. No one could prove how either functioned, so how were they very different? From the point of view of the modern sceptic, herbs remain the most effective form of ancient magic because the effects (in many cases) can be repeated and reduced to formulas that even the most un-magical individuals can use effectively.

Love potions Witches approached by lovesick clients would brew potions or use herbs in amorous spells. These were also effective, though arguably they worked because the users believed that they worked. Confidence is a great aphrodisiac. If a potion inspired that confidence, then it was indeed effective. Likewise, informing someone that they were under the effects of a potion could work as a strong disinhibitor, giving subjects an excuse for behaviour they'd rather like to indulge in anyway. We'll look at love potions in more detail in Chapter 3.

To illustrate the power of belief in drugs, known as the 'placebo effect', in a controlled experiment, a group of college students were informed that they had consumed a beverage that contained a measure of alcohol, when in fact it did not. Another group were actually given that same small dose of alcohol in a drink, but not

---

An odd herbal recipe

This magical recipe is typical of many surviving spells. They were written as reminders for a practising magician, rather than as instructions for a neophyte. So exactly what to do with the recipe when it has been brewed or what a shadow can do when under 'control' are matters that await rediscovery.

> To gain control of your shadow to make it serve you, prepare an offering of ground wheat, ripe mulberries and unboiled sesame, and uncooked *thrion**. Mash this into beetroot.[6]

---

* Perhaps fig leaves.

informed by the researchers that it was there. The first group showed signs of tipsiness, while members of the second group remained completely sober.[7]

Poisons There was no placebo effect at work in the administration of these concoctions. They definitely worked. It takes time, effort and privacy to cook up a good dose, but an expert can persuade even apparently innocuous fruits such as apples, apricots and cherries to become lethal. (These fruits contain a compound called amygdalin, which turns to cyanide in the human digestive system.) One witch made her name by putting such skills to 'good' use (see pp. 57–60).

Magical attractants and deterrents The right plants could attract magical beings or repel them. Even today the relationship between garlic and vampires is well known. The right herbs rubbed on a doorpost or placed on the threshold of a house could encourage or prevent access to the premises by certain creatures such as Lamias (proto-vampires) or lost spirits. Some magical spells recommend placing a posy of flowers on the grave of an individual to encourage that person's spirit to perform a magical task, for no other reason than that the dead like flowers (as a visit to any modern cemetery will demonstrate).

INCANTATIONS AND OTHER SPELLS

A spell is a formula that, when followed properly, produces a particular result. It differs from a recipe only in that cooks seldom invoke gods and demons (well, not formally, anyway), and in that the ingredients are generally more exotic.

An incantation is spoken – or rather, chanted, as the word comes from *cantare*, the Latin verb meaning 'to sing'. Long incantations,

This spell book from Egypt is called the *Handbook of Ritual Power*.
It contains twenty-seven spells, including fertility spells
and spells to confront demonic possession.

which often feature a recurring line, can have a semi-hypnotic effect, especially if the mind of the subject is already prepared through a suitable atmosphere, and the use of hallucinogenic herbs or soporific substances, or both. Again, whether incantations work is a matter of perspective. Incantations could be used to summon magical beings, enhance a potion, or be used in connection with other activities such as dance or prescribed gestures to create a spell. Numerous examples will be found in the following chapters.

A simple incantation

To test the power of incantations, try this spell for summoning the god Morpheus. After consuming the appropriate potion (ground cocoa beans in warm milk), readers should softly chant 'One white sheep, two black sheep, three white sheep, four black sheep,' and so on, until Morpheus, the god of sleep, comes to claim them.

The thing about spells is that they have to be done exactly right. With an incantation, even a pause at the wrong moment may be enough to sabotage the conjuration or produce unexpected side effects. The Romans knew this, which is why in their religious ceremonies even the most minor mistake meant that the entire ritual had to be started again from scratch. Just as with her pharmacopoeia, the prospective witch must learn an entire grimoire of spells before claiming any sort of mastery in the craft. Even Medea, the greatest witch who ever lived (see pp. 67–71), spent most of her teenage years in study.

'EXTREME' MAGIC

Forcing rivers to reverse their course, pulling down the moon and making forests walk or crops move from one field to the next are all feats attributed to witches in antiquity. A really *good* bad witch could also bring about storms, floods, hurricanes and other extreme weather events.

These are all feats that we may regard as public relations by magic-users, or hysteria on the part of the magically challenged. As the biographer and philosopher Plutarch (AD 45–127) cynically remarks of a witch called Aglaonice, the best time to 'pull down the moon' is when careful consultation of astrological tables informs the practitioner that the moon is going to disappear for a while anyway. Thereafter, a peasant gawping as an eclipse slowly wipes the moon out of the night sky might well imagine that some witch has stolen the moon for her own nefarious purposes.

In the same way, rivers do occasionally reverse course, usually as a result of erosion sediment deposits forming natural dams or avalanches blocking water flow. It was not hard to accredit such major landscape events to magical activity. Likewise, there are numerous stories of individuals who can somehow control the weather and make it rain. Once, a city suffering drought was so desperate for rain that it hired such a professional, with the proviso that he would only be paid if the local reservoirs were filled. So heavy were the resulting rains that dozens of people were killed in the deluge. Fearful that they would be considered responsible for the deaths if they paid the rain-maker, the city authorities refused to part with the promised payment. Rain-making is not confined to ancient superstition; the 'pluviculturist' in question was a man called Charles Hatfield, and the city was early 20th-century San Diego, California.

ARE WITCHES BORN OR MADE?

While it is clearly possible to learn many parts of the witch's craft through nothing but hard graft and dedication, it's also true that if one hopes to perform magical rites, it helps to be born with some magical talent. When we look at the most famous (or infamous) witches of myth, we discover that they were – at best – only partly human. With Circe, for example, we discover that the lady with a penchant for turning men into swine is actually the daughter of a god – the sun-god Helios, by some counts, the witch-goddess Hecate by others. Since either of these putative parents is divine, it should

A cartoonish Circe confronts Odysseus on this Boeotian pot.

come as no surprise that Circe was a skilled magic-user, and that her children in turn were magically talented.

The fact that there is a genetic element to the successful use of magic might appear discouraging for normal mortals, but in fact this is good news. The most common type of ancient divinity was the Titan, a species that included gods, such as Zeus, Athena and Hermes. Titans and humans are perfectly capable of interbreeding; Zeus, for example, proved this point with so comprehensive a legion of human lovers that he is one of the few individuals in any universe with the questionable honour of being his own great-uncle. Achilles, Hercules, Theseus and most of the other heroes of Greek and Roman mythology are in fact divine–human hybrids, and in the case of Achilles we have proof that humans could also interbreed with nymphs, his mother being an immortal Nereid.

Given that around three thousand years have passed since the Heroic Age, it is probable that much of the human race has in its veins at least a dash of the blood of Titans, nymphs or other magical beings. (Obviously, the more closely an individual can trace an ancestral connection to Greece, the less diluted that dash might be.) After all, the descendants of Genghis Khan (c. AD 1162–1227) have been breeding for far less time than the human descendants of the Greek gods, yet a 2003 study investigating Y-chromosomal lineages showed that over 16 million men now possess genes inherited from the Mongol warlord.[8] Hercules alone had well over a hundred children who also bred prolifically, so it is entirely possible that somewhere on the upper branches of your family tree perches Medea – a magical aunt fifty times removed and a hundred generations away.

So if the ability to perform magic is inherited, and the chances of being a distant descendant of the gods look good, then genetics could be no impediment to a spell-caster's success. On the other hand, no one should be too downcast if a spell fails. It just means that they are only human, after all.

THE TOP FIVE MAGIC-USERS OF
ANTIQUITY AND MYTH

The magic-users here fall into two categories. There are three well-documented individuals from Rome who certainly existed (though their powers may have been exaggerated over time), and two from the mythological era before history. Perhaps the fact that the latter two were the most powerful is unsurprising. The Greeks and Romans believed that theirs was the last age of the world, and magic was not as potent as it had been when the world was young.

5. Simon Magus, the flying sorcerer, AD c. 12–65

Much of what is known about this controversial character is confused and contradictory. The account presented here is not therefore 'the' life of Simon Magus, but 'a' life – the version that seems to make the most sense based on the conflicting evidence we have. A great deal of what we know of Simon Magus comes from the apocryphal gospels or 'Apocrypha', books that were once considered a part of the Bible but were later rejected after stern theological examination.

All historical sources agree that Simon was born in the Levantine province of Judea during the early years of the Roman Empire, and that he was a sorcerer who, according to the *Acts of the Apostles*, had 'bewitched the people of Samaria'. Simon was tempted by Christianity not because of his spiritual beliefs, but because he envied the powers that had been granted to the Apostles, such as healing the sick and speaking in tongues. He accordingly went to St Peter and asked to be given the same powers in exchange for pots of money. St Peter did not take the offer well, and said unto him, 'Let your money perish along with you for thinking that the gift of God can be purchased.'[9]

Rejected by St Peter and the Christians, Simon made his way to Rome, which at this time was ruled by the emperor Claudius. It was

The four-demon-power chariot of Simon Magus prepares
to take a tumble in this Renaissance engraving.

the centre of the world, and therefore – since Simon was nothing if
not an egoist – the only suitable venue in which to display his magical
talents. Once there, Simon took up with a woman called Helen, who
like her namesake, Helen of Troy, could whip up a decent potion
should the need arise. Simon preached his own doctrine, in which he
claimed that his Helen had actually *been* Helen of Troy, and before that
a divine being even more spiritual and greater whom jealous angels

had imprisoned on Earth and degraded over successive generations, and Simon himself was the holy power who had come to save her.

In the name of that divine power, Simon performed a number of magical acts, the specifics of which are now lost. These were apparently impressive enough for a cult of 'worshippers of Simon' to persevere throughout antiquity. According to the 2nd-century historian Justin, Simon's followers raised a statue to him on the Tiber Island, though more probably an existing statue of the largely defunct Sabine god Semo Sanctus was rededicated. (The similarity in names would make changing the inscription relatively easy.)

The cult of Simon quickly came into conflict with the doctrine of the Christian evangelists who had also been attracted to Rome. St Peter and Simon repeatedly clashed in theological debate. According to the Apocrypha, Simon tried to take the argument right to the top by appealing to the emperor Nero, who had by then succeeded Claudius. By his magical powers, Simon managed to fly high into the air over the Roman Forum in an enchanted chariot (one of the very few cases of levitation described in the ancient sources). Below the flying chariot, St Peter and St Paul – who had by now also arrived in Rome – prayed earnestly for Simon's literal downfall. Arnobius of Sicca (AD 250–330) described the scene:

> They saw the chariot of Simon Magus blasted into fiery
> fragments by the prayers of Peter, and vanish altogether
> at the name of Christ. I tell you, they saw him abandoned
> by his false gods in their terror. They saw him lie prostate,
> his legs broken by his own weight when he fell.[10]

Not only did the combined prayers of the Apostles bring the high-flying sorcerer down to earth, but they brought Simon so low that the fall killed him. Such was the force of these saintly imprecations that the knees of the Apostles left imprints on the paving stones on which they knelt. Visitors to Rome might like to drop into the church on the Piazza di Santa Francesca, next to the Forum. The stones are still displayed there, and visitors can study for themselves the dents that those knees made.

As to what became of Simon Magus, by the account of Hippolytus of Rome the magician was severely injured, but not killed, by his fall.[11] In this version of events, Simon ordered his followers to bury him in a grave that he had prepared in advance. He claimed that in three days he would arise again, restored to perfect health. The three days became four, then five, and the over-optimistic Simon remained firmly underground. Eventually, his disillusioned followers decided to let sleeping sorcerers lie.

4. Locusta, the fatal pharmacist, AD c. 5–69

In the year AD 54, around the time that Simon set up his stage in Rome, Agrippina the Younger, the wife of the emperor Claudius, had a dilemma. Though her son, Nero, was officially Claudius' heir, the emperor had another son, called Britannicus, who was also a potential successor to the imperial throne – and thus a threat to Agrippina's power. The historian Tacitus (d. AD 117) explains both the problem and the solution.

Agrippina had long ago decided to murder her husband.
She was unsure only of what type of poison to use.
A poison that worked instantly would betray the murder by its very suddenness. On the other hand, a poison that caused a slow, lingering death might cause Claudius to suspect treachery, and therefore return to his love for his [other] son.
What was needed was some rare *pharmaka* which brought death slowly, but deranged the victim's mind in

the meantime. Fortunately she was able to select an expert in such matters. This was Locusta.[12]

Tacitus says that Locusta had already been 'a tool of the tyranny', suggesting that on previous occasions the poisoner had been called on to discreetly remove enemies of the regime. However, when not serving as an imperial hitwoman , Locusta worked as a general poisoner for hire, and when the government was not there to make sure that no one asked inconvenient questions, she occasionally fell under suspicion. When Agrippina had need of Locusta's services, she had first to free her from the authorities, as she was already under arrest for killing another victim, not wisely but all too well.

There is a general belief that Locusta poisoned mushrooms to kill Claudius, but the skilled herbalist had no need to go quite that far. Instead she need only select two different – but almost identical – variations of the *Clitocybe* mushroom. One form of the species is edible and delicious. The other tastes just as good, but contains the deadly neurotoxin muscarine. With the help of a traitorous food-taster, Locusta arranged for both versions of the mushroom dish to be served at the imperial table.

It took a certain degree of faith for Agrippina to eat her portion of mushrooms while her husband beside her piled into an identical platter. As the journal *Scientific American* boldly announced in 2001, 'Case closed: Claudius Killed by Mushrooms'. Yet, despite the fact that Claudius' reported symptoms exactly match both Agrippina's requirements and the symptoms of muscarine poisoning, many nevertheless believe that Claudius died of *una uxor nimis* (one wife too many).

With the successful dispatch of Claudius, a grateful Agrippina arranged for the dropping of all charges against Locusta and the purchase of a large country estate, to which the newly crowned Nero would send students of the art of poisoning to learn their craft at the

'Then you see, the agonizing pain moves to the liver...'
Locusta demonstrates a new potion to Nero.

feet of the master. When there was a major case on hand, Locusta was called back to Rome to prepare the potion personally. One such case was the need to remove Britannicus, the rival heir and now a potential threat to the reign of Nero. The biographer Suetonius (AD 70–126) takes up the tale.

> He [Nero] ordered the arch-poisoner Locusta to prepare the potion. When it did not work as fast as he wanted, he called the woman to him and personally flogged her, saying he wanted Britannicus poisoned, not purged. (The previous dose had healthily emptied Britannicus' bowels.)....
> He forced her to mix the fastest-action poison in her collection, right there in his room under his eyes. He tried the dose on a kid, but the animal lasted five hours.

The mixture was distilled and purified again, then fed
to a pig, which instantly dropped dead. Thereupon Nero
ordered the mix to be taken to the dining room.[13]

There was the issue of Britannicus' food-taster, for after his father's
demise the rival heir had developed a healthy distrust of dinner.
However, an apparently inept server gave Britannicus a beaker of
water insufficiently chilled, and the princeling incautiously asked
for another…

Nero tried to pass off the prince's sudden death as an epileptic fit.
But a rainstorm drenched the corpse on the way to the funeral pyre,
and washed off the make-up with which the corpse had been lavishly
painted, Consequently the appalled public could see the blotched
and cyanotic skin that betrayed Locusta's handiwork.

Locusta continued her career of infamy, but like her protector
Nero, her days were numbered. Nero fell from power and, too afraid
to take the potion Locusta had given him in a jewelled box for just
that eventuality, died by the dagger. Locusta herself was promptly
executed by the new regime (though the idea that the execution was
accomplished through rape by a specially trained giraffe is a bizarre
modern fantasy, mentioned in no ancient source).

It may be argued that Locusta has no place in a list of distinguished magic-users, because her 'powers' amount to what we
would simply call 'chemistry'. However, this is to miss the point.
To the ancients, medicine *was* magic. Aphrodisiacs, contraceptives
and potions (both deadly and healing) appear equally frequently
in magical and medical textbooks – insofar as those in the ancient
world distinguished between the two at all.

3. Thrasyllus, who made a fortune from fortunes,
?–AD 35

No one was quite sure where Thrasyllus came from; he was Egyptian, certainly, but his origins were otherwise obscure. Of course, this obfuscation was deliberate, for Thrasyllus was a skilled astrologer. As the casting of a personalized horoscope requires the essential information of the alignment of the stars above the subject's birth, not knowing the subject's place, or for that matter date, of birth throws a fatal wrench into the whole complex proceeding. The man who made his name by divining the future of others was evidently reluctant to have the favour returned.

'Mighty first-begotten with wings of gold...' Eros Phanes, first of the gods, emerges from the world-egg surrounded by zodiacal signs symbolizing the cosmos.

Thrasyllus was no mere fortune-teller, but a scholar and a gentleman. He could talk learnedly on Greek grammar and expertly critique contemporary literary texts. Somehow he knew that a man named Tiberius, the future emperor of Rome, would fall out with his wife, Augustus' daughter, and end up in self-imposed exile on the isle of Rhodes. Accordingly Thrasyllus went to meet Tiberius there.

He attached himself to Tiberius' retinue through his knowledgeable discussions of Stoic philosophy, but what mainly drew Tiberius to Thrasyllus was the astrologer's certainty of a bright future ahead for both of them. Thrasyllus insisted that despite Tiberius' current unpopularity with the emperor Augustus, and a number of other heirs ahead in the queue, it was Tiberius who would be the next emperor.

Hobnobbing with the powerful had huge potential rewards, but also very real risks. Balancing the two took skill and timing, and here Thrasyllus' prophetic abilities kept him one step ahead. For example:

> This was precisely the time when Tiberius became
> convinced of the powers of the astrologer Thrasyllus…
> [It happened because of this…]. The pair were strolling
> along a clifftop, and Tiberius had decided to push
> Thrasyllus into the sea. Things were not going well for him,
> and he now regretted confiding so much in a man who had
> proven a false prophet.
>   At that moment Thrasyllus pointed at a ship as it
> appeared, and announced that it brought good news.[14]

Indeed, the ship carried messengers informing Tiberius that he was restored to imperial favour, and recalled to Rome. When, not long later, Tiberius did indeed become emperor, Thrasyllus enjoyed a prosperous career as court astrologer for his grateful client and eventually married a princess from the kingdom of Commagene in Asia Minor. While not casting horoscopes for his emperor, Thrasyllus indulged in academic study and produced analyses of the work of philosophers such as Plato.

He died assuring Tiberius that the emperor had a long life still ahead of him, thus convincing Tiberius that he would survive any current plots against him. Like any emperor, Tiberius was deeply suspicious that his appointed heir might develop premature ambitions, so this prophecy may well have saved the life of Tiberius' heir, Caius Caligula (with whom Thrasyllus' daughter was allegedly having an affair).

Tiberius Claudius Balbilus, Thrasyllus' son, also in his turn acted as court astrologer, deftly stepping around the political pitfalls involved in serving emperors as diverse as Claudius, Nero and Vespasian. It was almost as if he could see trouble coming.

2. Circe, maker of chauvinist pigs, the distant past–??

At this point, we need to distinguish between magic and sorcery. To the ancients 'magic' was the process of manipulating natural forces that the user does not fully understand. As the medieval writer (and magician) Paracelsus (1493–1541) says, 'magic is full of natural secrets'. Indeed, Paracelsus argues that the better we understand nature, the more capably we can manipulate magic.

So magic is basically the manipulation of (imperfectly understood) natural forces. Sorcery, on the other hand, is the essentially unknowable. It involves dealing with powers and personalities that are not of this world. Those who practise sorcery cannot hope to understand how or why a spell works when it is cast. One simply performs the required actions by rote, and hopes for the best. Sorcerers, to bring Paracelsus into the digital age, are the 'script kiddies' of the magical world, making use of pre-existing codes they do not understand or craft themselves:

Were the foundations of [sorcerous] art more closely
investigated by men, it would be seen that it was a hoax
of the spirits....Even if men arrived at perfection in this art,
what solid advantage would it confer?[15]

Circe was not only goddess of her art, she was also a skilled practitioner. Those who consider the genetic element crucial to witchcraft
and sorcery will note that Circe comes from the most magical family in
myth. Later writers, such as Diodorus Siculus (90–30 BC), assumed that
Circe's mother must be Hecate, the witch goddess (see pp. 99–102).[16]
However, sources such as Hesiod, writing half a millennium earlier,
are probably more accurate when they call her the daughter of Helios
(the sun) and Perseis, herself daughter of Oceanus (the sea).

The siblings of Circe were King Aeetes (see p. 68) and Pasiphae,
who married King Minos of Crete. Pasiphae was also a skilled magic-user, who forced her royal husband into fidelity – whenever he
had sex with another woman, the spellbound King Minos ejacu-
lated a painful mix of scorpions, spiders and centipedes, which was
invariably fatal for his lover. (It was perhaps a bit hypocritical of
Pasiphae to thereafter become enamoured of a bull, and give birth
to the Minotaur, but that is another story.)

Circe herself lived far to the west, on an island somewhere between
Italy and Spain. She was a recluse who had an arbitrary way with
sailors who stumbled across her island. The most famous encounter
between Circe and humanity came with the arrival of wandering
Odysseus on the sorceress's island, Aiaia. The isle was thickly wooded,
so Odysseus and his adventurers drew lots to decide who would
investigate the smoke coming from the glade in the centre of the
island. Odysseus describes their encounter with 'the goddess with
braided hair, who speaks to humans but has strange abilities':

Outside [her house] were lions and wolves which Circe had
bewitched with magic drugs....My men were shocked by the
sight of these massive animals. But they pushed on because
within they could hear the lovely voice of Circe with the
braided hair.

Circe invited the men inside her house and gave them food and
wine – both laced with insidious potions that caused the men to
forget their homeland.

Then she suddenly struck them with her wand, and they
became swine – snouts, bristles and all, though in their
minds they were still men. They sobbed as they were
penned up and Circe threw acorns on the ground for
them to eat.

Only one suspicious crewman had remained outside, and he
hurried to Odysseus with the news. As Odysseus hastened to the
rescue, he was met by the god Hermes (see pp. 97–99), who offered
some helpful advice:

On this 6th-century BC black-figure drinking cup, Odysseus enters on the left
to meet Circe while his second-in-command, Eurylochus, exits stage right.

I will tell you of her witch's arts. She will prepare a potion
for you, beneficial but for the drugs mixed in as well. Yet if
you take this antidote I will give you she won't be able to
ensorcel you.

Thus immunized to Circe's spells, Odysseus was able to charm the
sorceress into bed, and the two developed a long-standing relationship
that was only ended by Odysseus' eventual desire to return to Ithaca
and his loyal wife, Penelope. Yet some stories say that in the end,
Odysseus returned to Circe, though Ptolemy Hephaestion, a scholar
of myth in the late 1st century AD, offers this intriguing alternative:

An Etruscan potion-maker had worked for Circe, but later
fled from her. To her tower, called the Tower of the Sea,
came Odysseus [elderly and at death's door]. She gave him
drugs that turned him into a horse, and kept him with her
until he died of old age. This is how the prophesy in the
text of Homer is resolved – 'At the sea shall you find the
gentlest of deaths'.[17]

The Odysseus encounter was but one episode in the long and
storied career of Circe. She earlier had a child by Poseidon, Ruler of
the Sea, as well as another three children by the mortal Odysseus.
Yet Odysseus himself was not fully mortal, for he was descended
from the helpful Hermes. Divine on both sides of the family, it may
be that the line of Circe yet lives on.

1. Medea – a witch in time slays more than nine
c. 1300–1210 BC

When it comes to the ultimate in witchery, the winning candidate requires mastery of the whole field of magic, from pharmaceutical preparations and the casting of spells to the control of demonic entities. On top of that, we look for a master manipulator of human psychology and an ice-cold, unflinching determination to persevere with magical measures, no matter how extreme.

Medea fits the description to perfection, and is therefore awarded the #1 spot in our list of ancient magic-users. This despite the fact that she had more character flaws than character, and never came to a town that she didn't have to leave in a hurry. She possessed a phenomenal ability to wreck the lives of those lucky individuals closest to her ('lucky' in the sense that their lives were merely ruined rather than terminated altogether). Had she not been a witch, Medea would merely have been a murderer who had totally lost her moral

Medea rejuvenates a ram that she had chopped into a cooking pot. This convinced King Pelias' daughters to unsuccessfully perform the same spell on their father.

compass. With magical ability as great as hers, Medea was more dangerous to have around than a tiger with toothache.

In the account that follows we see expert chemical and pharmaceutical skills, demonology in the mastery of dragons, and deft psychological manipulations spoiled only by the manipulator's total lack of empathy. Interestingly, despite Circe being her aunt, Medea seems to have steered clear of the spells of sorcery.

Medea grew up in Colchis, a small kingdom at the back end of the least fashionable part of the Greek world – the eastern reaches of the Black Sea. Medea's father, the King Aeetes, was in the habit of arbitrarily slaying visitors on the off-chance that they had come to filch the kingdom's most prized possession – the famed Golden Fleece of song and legend. To while away her teenage years, Medea turned to witchcraft, and through natural aptitude rapidly became master of her craft (and by some accounts also a priestess of Hecate).

When a young hero called Jason appeared in search of the Fleece, the king was impressed enough by the young man's ancestry and family connections not to slay him immediately. Instead he set Jason the sort of tasks that would result in an instant (but entertaining) death that could not be directly blamed on him. That is, the tasks were deadly – unless the hero somehow obtained magical protection of the highest level. Of course, it was Medea who provided that protection, as she saw in the handsome young adventurer not just a suitable mate, but also her ticket out of the backwater she was stuck in.

So when Jason was challenged to sow dragon's teeth in a field with a plough drawn by fire-breathing oxen, Medea had a fireproof ointment on hand. When the dragon's teeth instantly sprouted into a field of homicidal warriors, Medea lobbed a completely unmagical rock into their midst. Unable to determine who had thrown the rock, the warriors blamed each other, and were all killed in the subsequent brawl. Then Medea provided Jason with a soporific drug to put to sleep the dragon that guarded the actual Fleece.

In this German woodcut, Medea uses the power of Hecate as
she exsanguinates the father of Jason (but in a good way).

Unsurprisingly, Aeetes took the loss of the Fleece badly, and set
out in hot pursuit of Medea and Jason as they fled Colchis. As usual
Medea, ever prepared, had brought along her little brother. Now she
killed and dismembered the boy, and discarded chunks of the corpse
at inconvenient places along her line of flight, forcing her father to
slow down to collect the bits for a decent burial.

At the island of Crete, the couple fell out with the invulnera-
ble Talos, a man of bronze. Realizing that a man who could not be
wounded could not heal, Medea maddened Talos with drugs and then
extracted an iron nail from his body. It was merely a matter of waiting
for Talos to slowly bleed to death before the pair made their escape.

They returned to Thessaly, Jason's homeland, and discovered that
Jason's aged father was hanging on to life by a thread. By exsanguin-
ating the old man and infusing his blood with healing herbs, Medea
was able to restore the father to youth and health. The daughters
of the king immediately demanded that Medea also perform the

same service for their healthy but ageing father. This was remarkably unwise, because the king had just reneged on his promise to step down from the throne in favour of Jason if Jason returned with the Golden Fleece.

The daughters meticulously followed Medea's instructions and chopped their father into dice-sized cubes. These they threw into a pot, and then they waited for a rebirth that never happened. Meanwhile, Jason and Medea fled town, with another murder to their name.

The pair ended up in the city of Corinth, where they lived unhappily for ten years. During this time Medea had two daughters. (Other versions of the myth credit the couple with up to fourteen children – practically superhuman in a single decade.) Then, perhaps tired of living on a volcano's edge, Jason announced that he was leaving Medea for the altogether safer Glauce, princess of Corinth.

Perhaps to Jason's surprise, Medea took the news well. She even prepared a beautiful wedding gown for her replacement bride. Modern experimenters have verified that it is in fact possible to saturate a dress with a sodium/phosphorus mix. Chalk dust inhibits the volatility of the compound, until it is ignited by the body heat of the person wearing the garment. For fashionable flare, the ideal dress should have seams lined with magnesium.

Because it is very hard to put out phosphorous, the king's attempt to extinguish his burning daughter resulted only in his own fiery death, and a shell-shocked Jason returned home to find the bodies of his daughters lying in a heap. Medea had killed them – and playwrights and psychologists still struggle to analyse her motive for the murder of her own children. It seems she was only waiting for the sadistic pleasure of seeing Jason discover his dead children before she fled town – this time on a stylish chariot drawn by flying dragons.

Eventually, Medea earned sanctuary in Athens by restoring the health of the king, whom she subsequently married. The couple had a son called Medeus (whom the historian Herodotus calls the father of the Medes, an ancient Iranian people). Then Theseus turned up. Medea immediately recognized the newcomer as the long-lost son of the king. Determined to preserve her son's inheritance, she brewed up a nice cup of poison for the visitor. Theseus was just about to enjoy his last drink when the king recognized the sword Theseus was wearing (he had left it with Theseus' mother), and knocked the cup from his son's hands. Then, once again, Medea had to leave town in a hurry.

By now, no one in Greece was mad enough to offer Medea shelter, so she returned to her father in Colchis. Aeetes was actually glad to see her, because he had been deposed from his throne in a palace coup. This was the sort of thing that a quick bout of Medean murder could put right in no time. The last reports from Colchis suggested that father and daughter were living amicably together in that faraway land, with Medea experimenting with immortality. One shudders to think of the consequences had she succeeded.

How did Medea manage to attract and keep such prestigious men on her side? Ovid offers a theory:

Medea trusts not her beauty or sweet character to make her sexy. She knows spells, and harvests fearsome plants with her enchanted sickle....She wanders through graveyards in a loose shift, her hair dishevelled, there to select choice bones from still-warm funeral pyres.

She uses spells to constrain her victims from afar, and makes magical dolls [kolossi] out of wax and shoves sharp needles into their suffering livers. I wish I could forget some of the other things which she does. Love should be produced by beauty and an attractive character. It is wrong to force it through potions.[18]

It is precisely this type of 'love' spell that we shall examine in the next chapter.

Ἔρως καὶ Ἔρις

THE MAGIC OF LOVE AND HATE

> Love-philtre, we've quantities of it
> And for knowledge if any one burns
> We keep an extremely small prophet, a prophet
> Who brings us unbounded returns.
>
> GILBERT & SULLIVAN, 'THE SORCERER'

Those who say that 'love is as old as mankind' are, of course, wrong. It is much older. In fact, the ancients believed that Eros, known as Cupid to the Romans, was the first of the gods to emerge from the primordial chaos from which all things were created. For without the reproductive force that Eros represents, how do you get more gods?

The goddess of love is Aphrodite, born of the sea-foam (*aphros* in Greek). She is of the generation before Zeus, King of the Gods, and Zeus too was born well before the first human. So magic-users who attempt to harness the power of love are dealing with one of the earliest primaeval forces.

Yet the foam from which Aphrodite (and her Roman counterpart, Venus) was born was created by the castrated body parts of Uranus, flung into the sea by his son, Cronos. With such conduct among the first gods, can we not say that hate came hard on the heels of love, and that the two are deeply intertwined?

Here we find that some spells to summon love are little different from spells of hate – the subject of the spell is cursed to suffer love just as he or she might be cursed to suffer illness or death. Often

Aphrodite is born from a cockle-shell (which symbolizes genitals,
in this case those of Uranus) on this early red-figure Athenian vase.

the spell was designed not to create love, but an erotic fixation.
(The Greeks and Romans had trouble telling the two conditions apart.)
Some scholars call this type of 'love' spell 'agonistic', and contrast it
with the gentler intentions of 'philia' magic, which was designed to
increase affection and companionship.

Here we will examine both types of 'love' spell, and the different
devices that the ancients employed to create desire. Then we will
turn to the spells of hate – those curses designed to ruin the lives of
the caster's enemies.

An alarming agonistic spell

This Greek effigy from the 4th century BC, discovered in Egypt, was made in the form of a woman painfully bound and transfixed with thirteen pins in the mouth, eyes and intimate body parts. Incredibly, this was part of a 'love' spell, intended to bewitch one 'Ptolemais, the daughter of Horigenes'. The caster urged a demon to:

> Drag her by her hair, by her guts, until she does not stand aloof from me...and until I hold her obedient for the whole time of my life, loving me, desiring me, and telling me what she is thinking.[1]

PHILTRA

We begin with 'philia' spells, one of the more gentle forms of magical coercion. Gentle perhaps, but the way to hell is paved with good intentions. Agonistic magic usually works by setting the agents of the Underworld (Hecate, Hermes or any of a host of demons – see pp. 95–105) to work on the psyche of the victim. *Philia* magic is more dangerous as it is usually applied directly to the subject, which can lead to disastrous results if things do not work as intended. Even the mighty Hercules died in agony from a tunic soaked in powerful poison. His wife had given it to him in the mistaken belief that it would make him love her more.

Of course, such methods did not exist only in myth. The classical biographer and essayist Plutarch (AD 45–127) recorded a case in which a man discovered what he thought was his wife's attempt to poison him. The accused woman put forward a heartfelt defence:

> Evil women envy us. It was fear of their magical
> concoctions and spells that led me to try to counteract
> them. I may be a foolish woman, but do I deserve death
> for preparing these love potions [philtra] and spells
> simply because I am desperate for more love than you are
> prepared to give me?[2]

Since quite often the difference between love and death was simply the size of the dose, the husband in this case would have had to think long and hard about the couple's relationship. Did his wife really want a more affectionate husband, or a dead one?

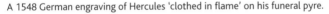

A 1548 German engraving of Hercules 'clothed in flame' on his funeral pyre.

A larger dose might not result in greater affection, but simply a quicker death. After all, unless the person administering the potion is an accomplished chemist and witch, she has to trust whomever gave her the potion or its recipe. A famous Athenian legal case involved a woman who killed off her stepson by persuading his lover to give him a large dollop of poison. The lover did this willingly, believing that she was administering a love potion. As the prosecutor informed the jury,

> But when Philoneos' mistress poured the wine…she poured in the poison with it. Thinking herself inspired, she gave Philoneos a larger draught, believing that if she gave him more, Philoneos would love her more. Only when the damage was done did she see that the stepmother had deceived her.[3]

These methods belong to the genus of love magic known as *philtrons*: love potions. Make no mistake – *philae* potions can be more deadly than *agonistic* invocations. The demons invoked by *agonistica* may or may not exist, and may or may not be compelled by the spell. But cyanide is very real, and it works every time.

Some *philtrons* are less magical than others. For example, we find faith in the seductive power of alcohol scratched on the Cup of Nestor – 'whoever drinks from this cup shall immediately be seized by the desire of fair-crowned Aphrodite', a sentiment matched 2,750 years later by the cynical 20th-century American aphorism 'candy is dandy, but liquor is quicker'.

The Roman poet Horace (65–8 BC) describes a truly evil *philtron* created by a witch named Canidia. She buried a boy up to his neck in the ground and then let him starve to death with food and drink just inches from his nose, so that his marrow and liver might become saturated with a helpless longing, to be transferred to whoever took the potion made from these body parts.[4]

THE FOOD OF LOVE

The Greeks and Romans believed that the vegetable kingdom yielded aphrodisiacs in abundance. In keeping with the ancient viewpoint, we shall not differentiate between those plants which aroused love and those which aroused sexual desire. As many a classical courtesan cheerfully pointed out, once you have awakened the one, it is merely a matter of technique to bring about the other.

We might consign aphrodisiacs to a different category from magic, but to do so misses the point – to the ancients, 'magic' and 'spells' could be as banal and everyday as the modern rituals of taking vitamins with a meal or cleaning your teeth afterwards. (The moderns believed that they had to stand before a mirror and rub bristles over their teeth. If this was not done regularly, they would lose their friends and their teeth would drop out.)

Having much else to include in this chapter, we shall cut right to the chase by combining some of the most reliable ancient aphrodisiacs into a single menu. This should lead to either a night of wild passion or a week of heartburn. The author disavows all consequences, physical, mental or moral.

In compiling this menu we have skipped the dangerous, such as essence of mandrake root (which contains toxic alkaloids); the overly exotic (have you noticed that you can never get a hippopotamus snout when you need it?); and the frankly disgusting – a part of the afterbirth clinging to a foal was much prized.

The ingredients here are high in vitamins, zinc and sugars, all of which contribute to a feeling of liveliness and well-being, and indeed scientists have recently argued that some of the chemicals in oysters are actually good for the libido.

According to Roman dietary lore, men should be served lettuce – a noted anti-aphrodisiac – along with their arugula by those who want to keep their dinner parties decent (giving a whole new meaning

WINE LIST

Main course

Red wine with a touch of fresh coriander[5]

or

Mature red wine with crushed yellow camomile[6]

Dessert

Lesbian raisin wine, so-called because the recipe – a sort of
proto-sherry – is from the Greek island of Lesbos

The grapes, not yet ripe in every part but tasting sour, are dried in
the sun for three or four days until the clusters are wrinkled. After
pressing out, the wine is placed in the sun in ceramic jars.[7]

(The writer Dioscorides says this wine is 'good for lustful women'.
He does not define what he means by 'good',
so you take your chances here.)

MENU

Aperitif

Summer savory (*Satureja hortensis*) base with raw oysters in spicy
sauce containing nettle seeds and pepper
(Recommended by Pliny, Ovid and Galen.)

Main course – mainly for him

Arugula (rocket) salad with beans, chopped eggs, nuts and
steamed carrots

(The medic Galen insists on the beans, as he theorizes that gas inflates
the male organ. Skip them if you are unconvinced. For extra pep with
the arugula, add the seeds, taking care to bruise them so that they
do not pass intact through the recipient's system.)

Dessert – mainly for her

Diced steamed apple served with strawberries dipped in aniseed
with a sauce of honey and crushed pine seeds
(Recommended by Dioscorides, Ovid and Pliny.)

Cupids at a wedding. Note the fruit (apples or pomegranates),
the leash, and that one Cupid holds a torch instead of a bow.

to a 'balanced meal'). Apples have the same effect on the fair sex as arugula on the male, to the extent that the lady should get aroused simply by having them thrown at her. This is why a Roman couple left a marriage ceremony lightly stunned by a shower of nuts and apples, rather as a modern couple leave to rice and confetti. The Romans sometimes added white wheat to the shower to suggest the reproductive power of seed, which also features on our menu.

While aphrodisiacs were useful to get people in the mood, magic could also be used to ginger up the male's performance. In a scene from his infamous *Satyricon*, the Roman author Petronius (AD 27–66) describes a 'patient' suffering from erectile dysfunction who goes to visit a witch. She also happens to be a priestess of Priapus, the fertility god who has given his name to the condition of priapism.

'He can't close the deal, not with a girl or a boy. He's got
a strip of wet leather where most men have a functioning

organ. What can you say of someone who can leave Circe's bed without any pleasure?' Oenothea shook her head....

'May I drop dead if I don't get him as hard as horn.'[8]

The 'Circe' referred to here is a woman renowned for her powers of seduction, making the patient's inability to perform all the more shocking. Petronius describes the drastic measures sought by his afflicted character, a rather confused mixture of magic and herbalism that included a nettle suppository and the administration of peppers and hot oils to the genitals. (Nettles are in fact a major ingredient in that notorious potion known to later ages as 'Spanish fly' – though the 'fly' is actually a beetle – so Petronius probably based his story on an actual rite.) Apparently these remedies were effective, but when his hopeful lover, Oenothea – who was something of a hag – wanted to try out her work, he made a run for it down the street, naked and screaming in terror.

THE ENCHANTMENT OF SIMAETHA

This is a complete *agonistic* 'love' spell, as described by a Greek writer of the 3rd century BC called Theocritus. This spell was used widely in the ancient world – elements of it have turned up in bas-reliefs (carved friezes), archaeological finds and magical amulets. The incantation, used by Simaetha, a magic practitioner from the Greek island of Cos seeking to revive the waning interest of her lover, Delphis, is to be chanted while turning a wheel of brass. This summons and constrains a wryneck – the Eurasian woodpecker. When enchanted, this bird ensures that magical spells hit their mark. As a result of this, the Greek name for the bird is better known than the bird itself – *iunx* is the origin of the English 'jinx'.

A wryneck awaits orders to go and jinx someone.

So shine fair for me, sweet Moon. My hymn is to you, placid Goddess, and to Hecate of the Demons, who makes the puppies cower as she goes about her business where the tombs are, or where red blood lies spilled. I hail you, Hecate, the awesome and dreaded! I beseech you to be at my side that this pharmaka be as potent as any of Circe, or Medea, or Perimede of the golden hair.

Wryneck, wryneck, draw him to me.

[First barley-meal into the fire!...On, on with the meal, and chant 'These be Delphis' bones I throw'.]

Wryneck, wryneck, draw him to me.

As Delphis has caused me pain, so I burn these bay leaves against Delphis. It crackles and see! It is gone, so not even ash remains. Even so, let Delphis be consumed by a flame of another kind.

Wryneck, wryneck, draw him to me.

This puppet of wax melts before Hecate, so and so fast,
you melt with love, Delphis of Myndus. And as this wheel
of brass turns by grace of Aphrodite, so turn, Delphis and
return to my door.

Wryneck, wryneck, draw him to me.

As the flames consume this bran, I call on you, Artemis!
You who moves the unbreakable stone at the door of
Death, so shall you move all else that is unmovable.

[Hear now, how the Gods howl in the streets. Certainly the
Goddess is at these cross-roads. Quick, beat the pan.]

Wryneck, wryneck, draw him to me.

See now! Though the waves be still and the wind be still,
the fiery pain in my breast yet rages. I still burn for him,
he who has left me neither a wife nor a maiden.

Wryneck, wryneck, draw him to me.

Three times this libation I pour. Three times, Lady, this
prayer I say. At this moment, be his lover a woman or a
man, let be forgotten that lover, even as Theseus once forgot
fair-haired Ariadne.

Wryneck, wryneck, draw him to me.

Horse-madness, Arcadian herb [*Hippobroma longiflora*],
you make every filly, every mare run raving in the hills.

Just so Delphis, shall I see you, raving at my door, drawn
from the embrocations of the wrestling-gymnasium.

Wryneck, wryneck, draw him to me.

This fringe taken from the cloak of Delphis I now shred
and fling it into the ravening flame.

Wryneck, wryneck, draw him to me!

[Then take the ashes from the fire, and in the light of the
moon smear them secretly on his door or window frame,
and spit on them as you do so, and say 'Dephis, it is your
bones I spread'.]

Wryneck, wryneck, draw him to me![9]

The violence in many ancient 'love' magics is rather startling.
Perhaps it is unsurprising that the results were sometimes more
gruesome than intended. The Romans thought that the famously
demented emperor Caligula went mad because his wife Caesonia
gave him a drug intended as a love potion that instead drove him
insane. The poet Juvenal enlarges on this idea:

One man supplies magical spells, another potions from
    Thessaly
With these a woman can weaken her husband's mind
(To the point where she can whack his buttocks with her
    slipper!)
That's why you lose your reason, and forget everything you
did before yesterday.

Even that's endurable, if you at least avoid raving madness
Like that infamous uncle of Nero [Caligula]
Into whose drink Caesonia poured the membrane
Ripped from the forehead of a newborn foal…

Less guilty were Agrippina's mushrooms which poisoned
   Claudius
They merely stopped the heart of a single drooling old man
While the 'love-philtre' for Caligula caused fire and havoc
And left the best men of Rome dead in a mangled heap.[10]

In a final argument against love spells and potions, Plutarch says more or less the same thing. He does not deny that the spells work, but rather that they fail in their ultimate purpose:

'Catching fish by poisoning the water is quick and easy.
But the fish so caught are mostly inedible and worthless.
In the same way, women can use love potions and spells
and so gain mastery over men through pleasure. But they
end up living with stunned and senseless cripples.'[11]

A witch's lament

No root or herb that in wild places secretly grows has missed my grasp
Yet there he dreams between his perfumed sheets, free of any mistress
Alas! Some clever sorceress by her [counter]enchantments lets him still
   walk free.
Oh Varus, you are still doomed to a life of misery
I shall find some uncommon elixir to make you return to me
And no Marsian spells will devote you to another
I'll brew something more potent, and pour a stronger dose
To overcome your disdain![12]

AGONISTIC MAGIC – BRING ON THE DEMONS!

For those for whom the mixing of potions held little appeal, there was always the option of working on the mind and body of an intended 'beloved' through the power of the spirits of the Underworld. By use of the proper spells and rituals, carefully selected demons would be compelled to bring the caster's subject to his door (the casters of *agonistic* spells were usually male, whereas brewers of *philtra* potions were usually female) with the poor woman already crazed with lust. 'Love' in the ancient world was either the gentle protective love of – for example – a mother for her child, or love of a crudely sexual nature. Modern anthropologists argue that romantic love, with its hearts, flowers and moonlight walks, did not really exist in the ancient world. Instead, it is a social construct which evolved in the Middle Ages. For the Greeks and Romans, romance was mostly about inserting Part A into Part B to make Person C.

Love was a violent process, an attack by the gods upon the minds of otherwise well-balanced individuals, and this violence is reflected in the enchantments employed by those wishing to inspire such feelings in the object of their affection. Even today there is a reflection of this in the portrayal of the god Eros, who holds not flowers and sweet foodstuffs but a bow and arrow.

This invocation, found in a clay pot with two small dolls which were partly melted together, represents such a 'love' enchantment:

Bring Euphemia, born of Dorothea, to me Theon, the son of Prechia.

Make her love me with lust, longing and rut. Make her mad with desire. Burn her limbs, her liver, her woman's body. Make her stop ignoring me...do not allow her to eat, drink, sleep or laugh...until she comes to me, wanton with mad lust, to give me all she has, and to obey my every wish.

Eros prepares to take down another victim.
Roman copy of a 4th-century BC Greek statue.

Laevina at Baiae

In ancient times, Eros carried a whip and a flaming torch in addition to
his bow and arrow, and those 'in love' imagined themselves burned – with
desire – by the torch and goaded by the whip to seek the company of their
beloved. Such was the experience of Laevina at Baiae, a seaside resort
infamous for its expensive debauchery. The violence of the imagery was
to some degree as stereotyped as the 'piercing of the heart' that Eros
the archer still regularly accomplishes today.

Laevina, so chaste as to rival even the Sabine women of old…
while taking the waters at Baiae fell into the flames of love.
She arrived in town a Penelope [the famously loyal wife
of Odysseus], she left a Helen [of Troy].[13]

By the holy names and the powers I have invoked make this happen, Now, now! Quickly, quickly!

It is clear that Euphemia was unimpressed with Theon before he cast his spell. Indeed, she might not have even known that he existed. Rather than attempting to remedy this through romance, or even seduction, Theon has opted for a drastic shortcut that denies Euphemia the option of refusal, summoning 'holy names and powers' – in this case, restless ghosts and the prematurely dead – to do his bidding. In fact, the longer Euphemia holds out, the more painfully tortured her life becomes. Theon's approach seems completely devoid of 'love', or indeed any other positive feelings for Euphemia. Even by the low standards of antiquity, *agonistic* love spells are conspicuous for their coercion and lack of consideration for the person being bewitched. 'Love magic' is not the correct name for these spells. In essence and intent, they are rape by magical means.

A GREEK SPELL FROM EGYPT

With wax or clay, make two dolls, one male and one female. The male should be as the war-god Ares, armed with a sword which he threatens to plunge into the female's neck on the right-hand side. Make her effigy down on her knees with her arms behind her back....

Take thirteen needles made of copper. Stab one into her brain while saying 'I pierce your thoughts [insert name of victim here]. Stick one needle in each eye, one in each ear, and one in the mouth. One goes in the belly, one in each hand, two in the genitals and one in the sole of each foot. As you do this, say each time 'I stab this part of her, so that with each stab she can think of nothing but me alone.'

Then take a lead tablet and inscribe the following spell upon it. Tie the inscription to the figures with a thread with 365 knots, and as you tie chant 'Abrasax, hold her fast!' Then at sunset, place the figures beside the grave of someone who has died suddenly or violently, together with an offering of seasonal flowers. The spell is as follows:

'I call on you by those names that cause fear and trembling, by the name which terrifies demons, the name which makes rivers burst their banks and causes rocks to shatter. I conjure you, Lord of the Dead, by Barbaritha Kenmbra Baroukambra, by Abrat Abrasax Barpharangges, by the glory of Mari…fail me not, Lord of the Dead, and send [some demon] whether male or female so search every place, every house for [insert name of victim here] and drag her to me.

Keep her from food and water, and keep her from seeking pleasure with any other man, even if he is her husband. Pull at her hair, pull at her heart and her soul, every hour of her life, every day and every night so that she must come to me, be with me, be inseparable from me. Bind her to me for all of my life, and force her to serve me. Let her enjoy no moment of peace away from me. Do this for me, Lord of the Dead, and I shall allow you to return to your rest.'[14]

This is a 'love' spell, yet in almost every way it is manufactured in the same way as a curse. The spell is inscribed on lead because, like gold, lead does not corrode (and is a lot cheaper). Therefore the spell remains inscribed on the lead and keeps its power. The grave of someone who had suffered a violent or unexpected death is chosen because the spirit is assumed to be restless. The ghost is therefore more likely to return to the earthly plane, and on his return to carry the message in his grave to the spirits of the Underworld.

Opening lines of a spell to bind demons where children are buried

Children, having suffered untimely deaths, were a favourite subject of conjuration. Once bound, the demon could be used for any purpose the magic-user desired. (It is uncertain whether this spell was to be written or spoken, and this uncertainty is probably deliberate. Accomplished magicians in the classical world disapproved of amateurs, and missteps in spells involving demons was probably seen as a good way of reducing their numbers.)

I bind you, demons with the unbreakable chains of the Infernal Fates. By mighty Necessity I conjure you by those who lie here, and are restless here and who still are busy here, those boys who have died too soon. By the unconquerable power of Iao, Barbathiao Chermari, rise up now, you demons who lie here![15]

Another feature of both curses and this type of love spell are the needles that put the 'agony' in 'agonistic'. Again, the difference here between love and a curse is only one of intent. With 'love' spells, the victim is intended to suffer lust and longing. With curse spells the victim is intended merely to suffer. Often the effigies being stabbed are made of wax, all the better for them to 'melt with love' in Eros's flames. Some inscriptions suggest that straw dolls were also used by those who preferred their subjects to 'burn' for whatever reason, but straw does not wear well over the millennia, and through their function most dolls were burned anyway, so the chances of finding any are slim.

Magic-users such as sorcerers and witches were also able to 'draw down the moon' (or Selene, the moon goddess), sometimes literally, sometimes metaphorically, to deposit a dew on prepared grass. This liquid made an effective love potion. Women from Thessaly were supposedly able to draw down the moon at will, though at a

Drawing down the moon. Selene descends in her chariot
on a Roman sarcophagus from Ostia, Italy.

terrible price. Every drawing cost them an eye, or the life of one of
their own children.

We see the drawing down of the moon, necromantic ritual and
magical dolls all combined to good effect in the 2nd century BC by
the irrepressible Lucian of Samosata (AD 120–92) in his *Philopseudes*.
Lucian describes a rich landowner called Glaucias besotted with a
girl called Chrysis. At huge expense – about 360 troy ounces of silver
– Glaucias hired a Hyperborean sorcerer to force the girl to satiate
his lust. (The Hyperboreans were a semi-mystical people from the
far north, beyond the known world.)

A witness describes to Lucian what happened next:

'First he [Glaucias] had to pay four minas to cover the
cost of the materials and sacrificial animals. He had also
to promise another 16 minas if the girl was successfully

Hecate holds enemies at torch-point.

bewitched. Then they had to wait until the moon began
to grow full, for this is the best time for such rituals.

Then at midnight the sorcerer dug a hole in the courtyard
of the house, and [by necromantic rites] called up the
recently dead father of Glaucias. The old man was angry
about the love affair, but eventually agreed to facilitate it.
After that there was a rite to summon Hecate, and she
came, accompanied by Cerberus. Then he drew down
the moon, and Selene took a number of different shapes.
First it was a woman, then an ox, and then a puppy.

After that the sorcerer fashioned a love-doll from clay
and said to it "Go! And return with Chrysis", and the clay
flew off into the air.

Soon after there came a banging at the door, and she was
there. Chrysis came in and embraced Glaucias, absolutely

insane with lust. She stayed with him in bed until the morning cock-crow. Then Hecate vanished into the earth and the moon flew back up into the heavens, and the other summonings faded away. Then we sent Chrysis back to her home.

If you had only seen these things, my friend, you would never again doubt the effectiveness of magic!'

I said 'Forgive me, that I do not have your keen eyesight. Indeed if I had seen these wonders then certainly I would believe. On the other hand though, I do know the girl Chrysis – and she is a randy little minx. If Glaucias had only asked nicely, he could have had her for twenty bucks.'[16]

SPELLS OF HATE: CURSES

Hecate of the Underworld, Artemis of the Underworld, Hermes of the Underworld, shower hate upon Phanagora and Demetrios, upon their tavern, and upon all their property and all that they possess.

In blood and ashes and by all the dead, I bind Demetrios, my enemy. The binding in which you are entwined, Demetrios, is as strong as can be. The four-year cycle will not release you, and I hammer your tongue with a *kyntos*.[17]

This is what we may term a commercial curse, for it was found with four others in the wall surrounding the grave of a young Athenian woman, all written on similar lead sheets and using almost identical language. In every case, those running taverns are targeted by the curse, so it seems very probable that the curses were inscribed for the benefit of a sixth tavern owner seeking to (literally) cripple the competition.

The 'four-year cycle' to which the tablet refers was a common one in ancient Greece, and is the reason why the modern Olympics, like their ancient counterpart, are held every four years. So either a spell is naturally weakened after four years, or events that took place every four years, such as the Great Festival to Athena, loosened the spell as a by-effect of the general rites cleansing and purifying Athens.

These curses are neatly written with such elegantly precise Attic Greek that scholars suspect a professional magical practitioner was taking dictation from a customer. However, the tavern-owner's feelings seem to have got the better of him toward the end, where the curse lapses into colloquial language: 'I hammer your tongue with a *kyntos*' is meaningless as a literal translation, but a *kyntos* ('dog's ear') was the lowest and worst possible throw of the dice, so it seems that the curse intended either that Demetrios become tongue-tied, or, more probably, that whatever he said brought ill-fortune. However, the word 'hammer' is no slang reference but a literal action. On completion of the curse the tablet was folded over and sealed with a nail hammered through it.

While every curse tablet has some unique features, the formulation in this collection may be considered a reasonably typical example

Roman curse against a woman called Tretia to 'mix her mind, memory, lungs and liver together'.

of the ancient curse, though one which is both particularly articulate and prepared with exceptional care. (For obvious reasons, many curse tablets were apparently made by people in the grip of strong emotion.) Similar tablets have been found across the Greco-Roman world, often deposited in the graves of the untimely dead, but also in wells, underground sanctuaries and in portals to the Underworld (see pp. 26–33). The important thing for the sender was that the inscribed messages reached the infernal powers.

THE INFERNAL POWERS

One reason the Greeks and Romans often opted to have their spell-casting done by professionals is because calling on the subtle and deadly infernal powers can easily backfire. By definition, the gods invoked in a curse are capable of inflicting pain, madness and excruciating death. Forcing them to do your bidding is rather like juggling nitroglycerine, except that nitroglycerine kills you relatively quickly and cleanly.

Because of this, there is this fundamental difference between love spells and curses. While hopeful lovers happily gave their name and parentage (and sometimes even their address, in case the demon was unsure where to dispatch an ensorcelled victim), much of the preliminary rites involved in casting curses are about comprehensively anonymizing the curser. (This works because the classical gods were neither all-seeing nor all-powerful.) The curser is almost always anonymous and as an added precaution may have sought out the assistance of a professional, who took on the risk of any magical slip-ups.

GODS OF THE UNDERWORLD

Academics call the Underworld gods the 'chthonic' deities (*chthonic* literally meaning 'subterranean' in Greek). They are many, and they are not interchangeable. Nor are all of them suitable for invocations for curses.

Hades/Pluto, Lord of the Underworld

The Greeks were reluctant to invoke Hades, ruler of the dead, in curses – presumably for the same reason that one does not call in the Chancellor of the Exchequer over a tax dispute. The man is too busy to be concerned with your individual case, and if he does decide to give you his full attention, he's going to make it worth his while in ways you will not appreciate. In the ancient world, temples to Hades/Pluto were few and far between. Attracting the attention of the Lord of Death, whether by prayers or curses, is seldom a good idea.

The Romans were somewhat less restrained than the Greeks in this regard, perhaps because they also could by tradition appeal directly to their emperor. For example, in 44 BC, when a concerned citizen wanted to warn Julius Caesar of his impending assassination, he slipped Caesar a note. Caesar assumed that the note was a petition, and so he tucked it away in his toga to read in the 'later' that never happened. So much was it the job of those in power to accept such appeals that when, a century and a half later, the emperor Hadrian told a woman with a petition that 'he was too busy right now', the woman snapped back 'Then don't be emperor!' A curse is, in essence, a petition, urging the divine powers to smite Person X in the name of truth, light and justice (as perceived by the curser). And if the Romans could petition the lord of this world, why not also the lord of the next?

Above: Hades enthroned, with pillar behind and Cerberus beside him.
Below: Hades and Persephone. Persephone holds corn, a symbol of life,
while Hades holds asphodel, a flower often planted on ancient graves.

Persephone/Proserpine,
(part-time) wife of Hades/Pluto

Just as the Romans were (slightly) more prepared to ask Pluto to smite their enemies, so they were more inclined to invite his wife Proserpine to join in the fun. The Greek form of Prosperine was Persephone. Though abducted by Hades and compelled to spend half the year in his shadowy realm, for the other half of the year she returned to the surface to begin the rebirth of the earth and bring the rains that awakened the seeds of the grain. As such, despite her connection to the grim Hades, Persephone is a goddess of new life and growth. This makes her altogether too benevolent to be of use to the serious curser, though she might be included in an omnibus invocation for the sake of completeness.

Hermes/Mercury

Hermes, on the other hand, is almost essential to a good curse. Today Hermes (or the Roman Mercury) is mainly – and wrongly – known as the messenger of the gods. In fact, the divine mail-carrier was Iris, the goddess of the rainbow whose arc spans heaven and earth. When Hermes does carry divine messages, these come directly from Zeus himself. This incidentally shows yet again the risks inherent in spell-casting. When, through the invocation of terrible names and binding offerings, you have commandeered Hermes for your own purposes, you might afterwards have to explain to the furious Lord of the Universe why you hijacked his mailman.

However, carrying messages for Zeus is something of a sideline for Hermes. As well as being the god of swindlers and businessmen (when these are not one and the same), this god is busiest as Hermes Psychopompos – Hermes, the Guide of Spirits. The ancients believed that when you die, the last thing you see on this earth is Hermes

Hermes with winged boots and and *kerykeion* (herald's staff).

Psychopompos, come to show you the way to the Underworld, where you will join the spirits of the dead.

These spirits of the dead are called *manes*. Roman tombstones are usually inscribed with the letters D.M., which stand for '*Dis Manibus*' – 'to the Spirits of the Dead'. Romans on a journey carried letters of introduction to show the people at their destination that they were persons of good standing. Tombstone inscriptions were basically the same type of letter for this greatest and most mysterious of journeys, and they commended the newly deceased to the residents of his new community.

The person who carried the message on the tombstone to the Underworld was Hermes Psychopompos, and while he was at it, he would also pick up from the grave any other mail addressed

---

An appeal to the dead

The text of a tightly rolled scroll placed in the grave of a man called Makron in Pella in ancient Macedonia in around 350 BC urged the spirit and his otherworldly companions to intervene in his marital interests.

> To Makron and the daemons of the Underworld, I entrust this scroll. Until I dig it up again and unroll it, let Thetima [my rival] not marry Dionysophon. He should take no other woman but me, and I should grow old with Dionysophon and no one else.

---

to the Underworld. This was in keeping with the usual method of sending mail in antiquity – in the absence of a postal service, mail was usually left at inns and other public buildings. Anyone going in the right direction could carry the letters further toward their destination if they were so inclined, rather as kindly folk today might pick up hitch-hikers. So in the classical era, if you had a message for Philothanatos of Cumae you would leave the letter at an inn on the Appian Way. If you were writing to Hecate of the Underworld, you left the letter in a fresh grave. Incidentally, Romans did not bury their dead within the city walls, so every road leading out of town had tombs on each side.

Hecate/Trivia, the divine witch

Hecate got a lot of mail. She is an interesting goddess, to whom 'mighty Zeus gives full honour'.[18]

> For as many as were born of Earth and Ocean amongst
> all these she has her due portion. The son of Cronos did
> her no wrong nor took anything away of all that was her
> portion among the former Titan gods: but she holds, as the

division was at the first from the beginning, privilege both in earth, and in heaven, and in sea [i.e. in the kingdoms of Hades, Zeus and Poseidon].

Classical mythology goes into great detail about the soap-opera lifestyle of the more dramatically inclined gods, but Hecate remains a quietly lethal presence in the background. She is a virgin goddess, which tells a lot about her in a pantheon where the senior male gods rape females – even family members – pretty much at will. Even among those dread powers, the unwritten rule was 'you don't screw with Hecate'.

Originally Hecate was a goddess from Asia Minor, but she was imported to Greece and Italy literally by popular demand. She has always been the 'people's goddess' – a supporter of the victimized and dispossessed. When Hecuba, wife of the king of fallen Troy, was surrounded by her enemies, Hecate saved the queen by turning her into a large black dog. This black dog became Hecate's familiar, and often presages her appearance. It is also why dogs howl when she is near, and why those wanting to get her attention sometimes sacrifice a puppy at a crossroads.

(Note that a 'crossroads' to the Romans was what today we would call a 'T-junction'. In many cultures a crossroads is considered a supernatural place, and Hecate was so closely identified with the crossroads that – an interesting bit of trivia – her Roman name means 'three roads'.)

Hecate is often shown with three bodies facing each point of the crossroads, an image that symbolizes her three-fold presence – in the heavens, on earth, and in the Underworld. When depicted as a goddess of the Underworld, Hecate carries two torches. As a goddess of the Underworld, Hecate has command of demons, and those calling down curses generally ask Hecate to select a suitable demon to do the deed.

Statuettes of triple Hecate were often placed in private homes.

The thing to remember about Hecate is that she is the last court of appeal for those who have failed to obtain any other form of redress. The goddess has a strong sense of justice, so it is dangerous to call on her unless you genuinely feel that you have been wronged. She is terrible against the unjust, so before you invoke her, be absolutely sure that when you have her attention Hecate doesn't decide 'the unjust' includes you.

Hecate may decide to grant a petition, but it must be phrased with care. Thus a witch informs a client who asked for a forbidden spell:

This Hecate forbids, for your request is unfair and unjust...
A greater spell [and different] I'll dare...
If the three-formed goddess will lend her aid
Then shall succeed this bold and awful enterprise.[19]

DEMONS AND *REALLY* MALEVOLENT SPIRITS

This is a good moment to clarify what is meant by 'demons', such as those whom Hecate and friends are often asked to send to help a magical petitioner. By and large, when the infernal powers are invoked, it is a demon who is expected to do the actual dirty work. Demons have a bad reputation because the Judeo-Christian tradition correctly associates them with the Underworld, but incorrectly associates the Underworld with Hell.

To the Greeks and Romans, a 'demon' was an Underworld power more than human and less than divine. Sometimes it might even be the spirit of a deceased hero. As the journeymen of the spirit world, these beings might be invoked directly, or manifest the will of a divinity such as Hecate. (This is why the programs that do a lot of the background work on the internet in fetching and manipulating data are called 'daemons.') The good thing about working with demons is that – although the Bible vehemently disagrees – demons are not inherently malevolent.

If, on the other hand, you want out-and-out nasty, call on the Daughters of Nyx (Night). To the Greeks these were the Keres or, as Homer more explicitly calls them, *Keres thanatos* – the Deadly Keres. The Romans called them the Tenebrae: the Ones of Shadow. While Ares/Mars, god of war, and Athena/Minerva, goddess of strategy, have a legitimate place on the battlefield, the Keres are just there for the blood.

The Ones of Shadow, gnashing their white fangs, scowling,
grim, bloody and callous, fought over those falling,
desperate to drink their dark blood. As a man was defeated,
or fell with fresh wounds, one would clasp him in a huge
claw as his spirit went to the Underworld....When sated
with that human's blood, they tossed him over a shoulder
as they rushed back into the tumult of battle for more.[20]

The Keres are also there, invisible and baneful, in earthquakes,
fires and other disasters. By and large, the Keres are avoided by
the average spell-caster because, in their sheer malevolence, they
might decide to take down not only the suggested victim but also
the person casting the spell. Safely commanding the Keres takes a
premier-league witch:

Her incantation sought to enlist even the aid of the Keres,
who feast upon the soul, the swift dogs of the Underworld
that are launched from the heavens against the spirits of
mortals...such was the grim power of Medea.[21]

Those browsing curse tablets should keep a special eye out
for Arentika, Anaplekte and Stygere. These are individual Keres
summoned by name, and therefore involve the sort of curses that
need handling with the spiritual equivalent of asbestos gloves and
long-handled tongs.

The Furies/Erinyes

Despite their fearsome name, the Furies are a safer invocation than
the Keres, should matters require their specialized attention. Though
even more ancient than the Olympian gods, the Furies are depicted
as serious young ladies, equipped with thigh-high boots and whips.

A Poena (a deadly spirit associated with the Furies) hovers over the altar where Medea has slain Jason's children.

Those who rather like that sort of thing will be disappointed to discover that to their victims, the Furies appear as hideous monsters, with snakes for hair, coal-red eyes and bat's wings.

The Furies punish those who commit crimes against family members (especially those of children against parents), and those who break a sworn oath. Because the latter category includes most senior public servants who swear an oath of office, the primordial Furies sometimes find themselves involved in very modern skirmishes between citizens and politicians. Rather as is also the case

The mythological hero Orestes on trial for killing his mother.
The Furies wait impatiently, held back by Athena (left).

with their better-known colleague Nemesis, the advantage of invoking the Furies is that it's their job to punish these misdeeds in any case. It's not even really a curse, since in appealing to the Furies one is merely being a good supernatural citizen and pointing out matters that need their attention.

NON-CHTHONIC GODS

Even though the 'heavenly' powers, such as Athena/Minerva, Artemis/ Diana and Apollo/Apollo, are not routinely invoked by curses, they may be called upon if a matter is within their jurisdiction. The gods have many aspects, and protect people under these. Demeter, goddess of the corn, was occasionally called upon to blight an enemy's crops. We have seen that Hermes was a patron god of travellers, and even the royal Zeus doubled as the god of hospitality. Therefore a dissatisfied modern holidaymaker might call upon Hermes to smite an unscrupulous travel agent and Zeus to deal with the hotel. (If the hotel offers fine wine at the bar, the lead wrapping around the cork is ideal for inscribing curses.)

SUPPLEMENTARY CURSE MATERIAL

While a written petition to the infernal powers is theoretically sufficient to secure their help, many ancient curse-casters supplemented their spells with visual aids, drawing diagrams or stabbing dolls with pins to helpfully point out the parts of the victim's body where suffering might be optimally achieved. (Not strictly necessary, but great stress relief.)

However, where the magical practitioner is not merely asking for the help of a god or demon, but *commanding* it through magical means, a little extra must be offered. That this is a high-risk enterprise goes without saying. Even in binding a demon, the magic-user is assuming the role of the gods. This is practically the definition of the excessive pride (hubris) that naturally attracts the attention of Nemesis – it's not hard to imagine how the gods feel about taking orders from a mortal. Alternatively, a binding spell could be used on a deceased spirit.

A curse constraining a demon to destroy a citizen of Cirta

This curse is accompanied by an image of the demon that the caster wished to constrain, a satanic-looking figure with prominent genitals and goat's feet. In a world where many people had only a single name, a good curse would identify the victim by both name and parentage to make sure that it struck the right person. The use of the more general phrase 'born of woman' (literally 'of a womb') in this example suggests that this curser lacked some vital information, and the terrible grammar of our barely literate curser makes it impossible to tell if Silvanus is the power charged with executing the curse or the victim of it.

> Seize him and make him insensible, without memory, or the ability to perform rites [to save himself?]. Empty his marrow, as I commit him, Silvanus, born of woman, to you. Take him and bind him...his deeds and his affairs. Kill him and deposit his soul in Tartarus.[22]

Binding spells often used *kolossi*, which were similar to modern 'voodoo dolls' in that they worked through sympathetic magic. What was done to the *kolossi* was magically transferred to the body of the persons with whom the *kolossi* were identified. Ideally, the doll should be made of lead or bronze, though wax and straw can be used also. Some material identifying the accursed should be worked into the figurine – a strand of hair, a fingernail or a scrap of clothing would do. Inscribing the victim's name on the doll is in any case essential. The doll should be transfixed with pins or nails at the points where the victim should suffer stabbing pain, and the head and/or feet should be twisted back to front, while the arms are bent behind as though the victim is bound. If death is demanded, then it helps to tightly confine the doll in a sarcophagus-like container.

After the necessary binding spells and invocations are performed, the doll should be placed in a fresh grave, preferably belonging to a

Witness intimidation, Athenian style. This doll in a lead box
was meant to harm enemies in a 5th-century Athenian trial.

dead bandit or murderer. In these extreme cases, the spell is not there
for Hermes to pick up, but to directly constrain the killer's soul to
do the deed. Demons can also be raised at the graveside by enlisting
the aid of the prematurely dead, including the spirits of children.
(It goes without saying that such antics in a modern cemetery will
deservedly invoke the wrath of the law even more swiftly than the
inevitable vengeance of Nemesis.)

Those intending the yet more dangerous invocation of a god need
to bury the doll in the appropriate sanctuary – hard to find nowa-
days – or in a body of water sacred to the god. Those commanding
Hecate have an easier job, because every crossroads is sacred to the
goddess, but rather like jumping off a cliff, 'easy' is not the same as
safe or advisable.

A CONSTRAINING SPELL BY AN ENEMY
OF CARDELUS

This Italian invocation is one of many curse tablets found in tombs along the Appian Way on the road from Rome. The 'god-nymph' appealed to in this curse, written on lead taken from a water pipe, may be Hecate, with Eidonea being an alternative spelling of [Hecate] Aidonaia (Hecate of the Underworld). People often believe that the foreign and faraway is more powerful than the everyday. This is also true of the gods and demons called on to execute spells. Deities invoked to command Hecate are the Egyptian gods Osiris and Apis/ Mnevis, the sacred bull of Heliopolis. The names at the bottom are the demons (referred to on the tablet as 'holy angels') whom the curser expects Hecate to use in executing the spell.

Osiris, Osiris Apis Osiris Mne Phri
    To you the god-nymph Eidonea…this ungodly tablet is
    entrusted, just as I also place into your hands the impious,
    accursed and doomed Cardelus, child of Fulgentia. Tie him
    to the rack to die a horrible death, Cardelus, whom
    Fulgentia bore. Do this within five days. I command you
    by the power that lies beneath the earth and controls the
    circles of the heavens.
    OIMENEBENCHUCH BACHUCH BACHACHUCH
BAZACHUCH BACHAZACUCH BACHAXICUCH
BADETOPHOTH PHTHOSIRO[23]

Myth and ancient literature are rich in tales in which love potions and curses are liberally applied. Archaeological discoveries such as this show that ordinary people were also fond of such magical coercion. Anyone tempted to emulate them should note that, in all these documented cases, hardly a single one ended well.

λυκάνθρωπους και στράγγοι

MAGICAL CREATURES

The ancient imagination was populated with strange creatures, from oddball people with one huge foot (which they used as a sunshade on hot days), to beings with faces on their stomachs, to huge, hairy and ferocious warrior women. (Actually this last was reported by an enterprising sea captain who seems to have ventured far enough along the African coast to capture a female gorilla.) The selection here is limited to those magical beasts with which we are still familiar today, though they, like our imaginations, have evolved slightly over the centuries.

VAMPIRES (LAMIA) AND OTHER BLOODTHIRSTY BEINGS

Modern fiction has familiarized us with the idea of vampires who form deep, romantic attachments with ordinary humans. The ancients had no doubt that vampires – of many kinds – existed. But though these creatures might pretend otherwise, their interest in flesh-and-blood humans began and ended with human flesh and blood. They might pretend to love humans, but really they just wanted them for their bodies. The experience of a handsome young man from Lycia named Menippos serves as a cautionary tale:

Depiction of a Lamia in a Renaissance woodcut from 1607.
Evidently the species had become less seductive since the classical era.

One day he [Menippos] was walking alone down the road
to Kenchreai [a port village near Corinth] when he met
a foreign woman, beautiful and delicate....

She told him that she was Phoenician, and had long
adored him from afar. She told him that she lived in
a particular suburb of Corinth, and invited him there.
'Come to me and I shall sing to you, we will have wine
better than you have ever tasted, there will be no others
to interrupt, and we shall be two beautiful people together.'

The 'romance' progressed over the following days, and the couple
planned to marry. As it happened, Menippos was a student of the
seer and miracle worker Apollonius of Tyana (AD 15–100), a man who

was not so much a magic-user as a sort of secular saint in his day. Apollonius saw right through the beautiful bride and told Menippos,

> 'This blushing bride is a Lamia....For them, love and the delights of Aphrodite are a preliminary used to deceive those upon whose human flesh they later wish to feast.'....
>
> At this the spirit pretended to weep, and begged him not to harm her or reveal who she really was. But Apollonius was relentless, and kept pressing her until she admitted that she was an *Empousa*, one of that species [of Lamia]. She was preparing Menippos through pleasure, so that she might later devour his body. It was her custom to seek out young and beautiful bodies to feast upon, for their blood was pure and strong.[1]

The Greeks and Romans easily understood the concept of vampirism, because – as we have seen in their necromantic rituals – they were firm believers in the magical power of blood. Blood was so important that the Greeks and Romans believed that an entire ecosystem of creatures existed on the substance, ranging from the humble mosquito to monsters that emptied entire bodies of blood at a single sitting. Some of these creatures were inhuman; some – like the *Empousa* described above – could pass for human; and others actually *were* human. Pliny the Elder tells us of the latter's dining habits:

> The blood of a gladiator is packed with life-force, and this they are in the habit of drinking. It horrifies us when we see this done by the wild beasts in the same arena. Yet, really, these human creatures think that this is the most effective remedy for their condition. That is, they put their mouth on the wound of a living, breathing human and drink the blood from it as though trying to suck out his very life.[2]

These desperate people were epileptics, who believed that human blood fresh from the vein could cure them of their condition.

> Blood, hot from the slit throat of a gladiator – that, they think, will free them from their disease. A wretched malady which they hope to make tolerable by more wretched means.[3]

If this Roman cure sounds bizarre, let us not forget that in 2018 there is at least one thriving business on the west coast of the United States that offers to rejuvenate elderly millionaires with blood transfusions from young, healthy Menippos-style males. If this is not actual vampirism, then it is certainly a way-station along the same road. In the Middle Ages, the Hungarian Countess Elizabeth Báthory (1560–1614) killed young women by the dozen, if not by the hundreds, and allegedly bathed in their blood to restore her youth. Human blood, it seems, has always been valued for its magical properties.

The idea that other – literally bloodthirsty – inhuman beings preyed on humans seems to have existed as long as mankind. An ancient Sumerian clay tablet in the Metropolitan Museum in New York[4] contains incantations to protect a priest from vampiric attack as he seeks to cure a patient, and the linguistic link between the original *Lemnutu* of Sumeria, the *Lamia* of Greece and the *Lemures* of ancient Rome confirms that our sources are discussing the same species of malignant spirit over a period of several thousand years.

Isidore of Seville provides a dubious etymology of his own, saying, 'Stories report that *Lamia* snatch children and tear them apart; and so they are named from *laniare*, "to rip"'. A child-orientated Jack the Ripper is chilling enough, let alone when we are talking of a whole species rather than a deranged individual. (Incidentally, the word 'lemures' lives on in the modern lemur – a small, monkey-like creature that evidently spooked early explorers in southern Africa.)

The Athenian playwright Aristophanes (*c.* 446–*c.* 386 BC) also mentions Lamia, but as a particular individual who gave her name to the entire species. According to ancient commentators on the text, this Lamia is related to an obscure myth in which she was a queen of Libya with whom Zeus had an affair. When Hera, Zeus's divine wife, discovered this, she reacted with her usual violence. (The 'seductions' of Zeus were generally rape, but, unable to punish her husband, Hera pioneered the art of blaming the victim.) Though in this case Zeus protected his lover, he could not prevent Hera from hunting down the offspring of the liaison, and killing them one by one. The Roman poet Horace (65–8 BC) hinted at an even more gruesome possibility – that Hera forced Lamia to eat her own children, when he described something in an obscure simile as being 'as impossible as extracting alive from her belly the child which Lamia ate.'[5]

Quite understandably, the whole ordeal turned Lamia into a deranged and violent creature. After her death she did not pass to the Underworld, but became a vengeful spirit who watched for unguarded children, killing any that she could get her claws upon. From this sordid and deadly beginning, *Lamia* became a generic term for any of the bloodthirsty undead.

One such creature was Mormo. We know little of Mormo, though this was the first vampiric being that most ancients became aware of. When they were children their nurses and mothers would assure them that if they were bad, Mormo would come in the night and bite them. (The effect of the bite probably depended on Mommy's imagination and how badly the children had behaved that day.) In Greek theatre, Aristophanes used Mormo as a sort of bogeywoman.

Summoning Mormo

The theologian Hippolytus of Rome (AD 170–235), though he did not believe in Mormo himself, quotes an incantation that summons her (use with caution):

> The enemy of light, and friend and consort of shadows
> Who revels in the howl of dogs when blood flows red
> Who walks among tombs and corpses turned to dust
> Who pants for blood, and freezes men with fear
> Gorgon and Moon, Mormo of many shapes
> Come to this, our sacrificial rite![6]

Hippolytus gives a number of tricks with which charlatans would enhance the ritual, but it seems that fire and darkness were important elements in the real ritual as well. However, all this does seem overkill for a summoning if one could simply encourage the children to misbehave during the day and then wait by their bedside at night.

THE NIGHT-FLYERS

They fly at night, their victims children yet unweaned,
Seize them in the cradle and defile their bodies.
With their beaks they rend the milk-fed flesh
And fill their throats with gulps of blood.[7]

While there was only one Mormo, Ovid describes an entire species of bloodsucking night-flyers. He tells the tale of an infant called Proca, but five days old, who was attacked by these proto-vampires. The creatures fed on the child's face and chest until his screams brought the nurse running. The child was found so drained of blood that, in Ovid's words, 'his face was the colour of leaves whitened by an early frost'. A magic-user called Crane was called to the premises. She quickly secured the nursery by rubbing leaves of *Arbutus unedo Ericaceae* (a flowering evergreen) against the door-posts and scattering them across the threshold. She then procured the intestines of a piglet – though from the incantation it appears that any very young creature would do – and offered them to the night-flyers with the following prayer: 'Birds of night, I offer a small creature in place of a small creature, a life given for a life more valued.'

After the sacrifice, the intestines were placed in the open, and a 'rod of Janus' was made from a branch of the white-thorn tree and placed by the nursery window. (Janus was the divine guardian of portals from whom we derive the month of January at the closing of one year and opening of another.) Ovid reports that the child was disturbed no more. Apparently appeased by the substitute, the night-flyers left him to make a full recovery.

THE UNDEAD

One argument against the death penalty in antiquity seems to have been that killing an evil person created a yet more malignant spirit.

> [They say] the souls of men are demons, and men become Lemures if they are bad....Who does not see at a glance that this is a mere whirlpool sucking men to moral destruction? For, however wicked men have been, if they suppose they shall become spirits they will become even worse. The more love they have for inflicting injury the worse they shall be. Hurtful demons are made out of wicked men.[8]

Over the centuries, the Lamia evolved in the magical mythology of antiquity. Some species became half-snake and half-human, while others were wholly seductive female humans whom Hecate sent to prey on unwary travellers. In the Middle Ages, the Lamia became the archetype from which evolved the succubus, the incubus, and, of course, the vampire.

WEREWOLVES

Moeris gave me these baneful herbs
From Pontus plucked,
Where dreadful plants abound.
Often I have seen him use them so,
To change himself from man to wolf
And then lurk, hidden in the woods.[9]

The story of the first werewolf is given thus: in the mythological Heroic Age of Greece, reports reached Zeus that Lycaon, an Arcadian king, was abusing his guests. To the Greeks the duties of a host were sacred, so Zeus, god of hospitality, donned a disguise and went to investigate. Lycaon suspected that his visitor may have been divine, so he devised a gruesome test. He took a hostage from his dungeons and killed the man, roasting some body parts and boiling others, and presented this grisly meal to Zeus. Zeus proved his divinity by instantly detecting what he was being fed, and he reacted with a divine fury that scattered the servants and sent Lycaon fleeing into the wilderness.

In a kind of madness, Lycaon turned his accustomed lust
for slaughter upon the flocks. As he took pleasure in blood,
his clothes became fur, and he started to walk on all fours.
So he became as a wolf, fierce as before with the same fury
in his face and grey hair.[10]

Lycaon transformed in this early Renaissance edition
of 'Metamorphoses' by the Roman poet Ovid.

While the ancients supposed the Lamia to be a separate species, and one somewhat higher up the food chain than humanity, lycanthropy was a rare but very human condition. The condition was particularly prevalent in Arcadia, presumably because once Lycaon had started the trend, others became more readily infected. One could contract lycanthropy by eating mutton from a sheep killed by a werewolf, so just as one is more likely to contract rabies in an area with a large local reservoir of infected creatures, becoming a werewolf was more likely in an area where werewolves abounded.

The 2nd-century AD Greek writer Marcellus Sidetes tells us how to identify, and cure, potential victims:

> They become pallid and listless. The eyes also become sunken. The tongue becomes dry, as do the eyes so they can no longer produce tears. They are continually thirsty but are unable to gain weight....

The treatment is to open a vein at the time when the affliction strikes, and bleed the patient to the point of fainting. After that give him a bath of sweet [herbs or unguents]. Wash him with whey milk daily for three days. Repeat.[11]

Given that the condition produces such debilitating symptoms, it is a wonder that anyone should voluntarily become a werewolf. Yet for some Arcadians, this became a rite of passage of sorts, as Pliny reports:

A man is selected by lot from the Arthus clan. He is taken to a nearby marsh, and there he undresses and hangs his clothing on an oak tree. He then swims across the marsh into the wilderness, and is transformed into a wolf.

He then seeks out a pack of others in the same condition, and lives with them for nine years....At the end of this period, if he so wishes, he swims back across the marsh, and retrieves his clothing. He then returns to his human form, though nine years older.

However, if the werewolf had tasted human flesh while transformed, the transformation was permanent, and he was doomed to remain a wolf forever.

Despite the fact that Pliny in his *Natural History* reports a number of somewhat more outré factoids, there is something about werewolves that seems to arouse deep scepticism among ancient writers. 'I can't believe the gullibility of the Greeks', fumes Pliny in this same passage (and admittedly it is a stretch to believe that clothing can hang on a tree for nine years without getting stolen). However, the very Greek Herodotus was no less sceptical:

> The Greeks who live in Scythia say that each of the Neuri
> peoples at some time becomes a wolf for a few days.
> Thereafter they revert to their human form. I personally
> am not convinced, but that's what they say, and they swear
> it is true.[12]

The Romans, of course, had a close connection with wolves. They believed that the founders of their city, Romulus and Remus, had been suckled by a she-wolf when they were abandoned to die as babies. The derogatory term by which the city's enemies referred to it was 'the wolf' – a title the Romans proudly accepted. Every year on 15 February the Romans celebrated the Lupercalia, a festival that was of such great antiquity even in classical times that most of the words were in an ancient form of Latin incomprehensible to listeners.

> In the ritual a goat and a dog were sacrificed, and then
> after a ceremonial meal, noble-born young men, and even
> Roman magistrates run naked about the city. They jokingly
> and amid much laughter strike those they meet with
> goatskin whips. Many women, even aristocrats, take care
> to be so struck believing that this is an aid to becoming
> pregnant.[13]

It is perhaps because of this connection with wolves that, according to some scholars, the Romans invented the werewolf, though they did not use the term 'werewolf', instead referring to such beings as *versipellis* – 'skin-changers'. The term referred to any shape-shifter, but especially to wolf-men. While werewolf stories tell of events dating back to the earliest times, apart from the brief mention in Herodotus given above, the first werewolf story in written texts was penned relatively late, at the start of the 1st century AD. (Tales of the Lamia, by contrast, go back almost as far as the invention of writing.)

Renaissance modesty has overclad the men in this woodcut of the Lupercalia;
the women and child are Cupid and personifications of fertility.

However, once werewolves were up and running (so to speak), the idea gained an unstoppable momentum. Evidently there is something in the human-wolf combination that appeals to the human psyche, for by the Middle Ages every European country had a respectable stock of werewolf legends, and a number of people had been tried in court and condemned for practising lycanthropy.

Werewolves make regular appearances in modern fantasy books and films, such as *Harry Potter and the Prisoner of Azkaban* and *Twilight*. In more recent lore there are several variations from the ancient accounts. The idea that werewolves are vulnerable only to weapons of silver is one, and another is that a voluntary transformation into a werewolf can be accomplished through wearing a wolfskin girdle. (Though the poet Virgil does have the sorcerer Moeris accomplish the change voluntarily, through potions.) Also, in the ancient sources there are no accounts of anyone transforming to a werewolf as a consequence of being bitten by one, though Pliny gives this account of an infection which comes close:

> Demaenetus of Parrhasia attended a human sacrifice
> that in those days the Arcadians still used to make to
> Zeus Lycaeus [Zeus the Wolf]. At that time he tasted the
> intestines of the sacrificed boy, and was turned into a wolf.
> He remained in that condition for ten years. Thereafter he
> trained as a boxer and later returned victorious from the
> Olympic Games.[14]

The Greeks and Romans did on occasion sacrifice humans, the latest instance being the Romans burying four people alive in 113 BC, according to Livy.[15] It seems that here the sacrifice was a lycanthrope (note that the location was Arcadia), and ingestion of his flesh committed Demaenetus to the same fate.

We also have an account of moonlight forcing the change from man to beast in the best of the ancient werewolf stories. Sadly, this is not merely fiction, but the outrageous and often bawdy fiction of Petronius' *Satyricon*. While this anecdote is therefore pure fantasy, it does give us something of the flavour of the beliefs circulating at the time. The narrator is travelling to meet his girlfriend, Melissa, who lived on a smallholding outside town. Travel on Roman roads was always dangerous, due to the threat of footpads, wild animals and, apparently, werewolves. Consequently, while passing the night at a local inn, our hero was glad to have found company for the next part of the trip, and even better, 'a soldier, brave as Orcus', Orcus being 'the Punisher' – a God who avenged broken oaths.

I took the opportunity of persuading him to accompany me as far as the fifth milestone. We got our backsides in gear and set out just before dawn, with the moon shining as bright as if it was midday.

When we got out among the tombs my companion went for a piss against a gravestone. I stayed put, humming to myself and idly counting the grave markers.

When I looked back for my companion, I almost died of fright. Certainly I became as immobile as a corpse. For he had taken off all his clothes, and folded them beside the road. Then he urinated in a circle around them. Then he became a wolf. No, seriously, he did. I'd not lie about this even for a rich inheritance.

As I was saying he became a wolf, and gave a howl and ran off into the woods. At first I had trouble recalling even where I was, but then I went over to pick up his clothes. But it was as if they were turned to stone.* If ever a man died from sheer terror, I should have done so right then. I drew my sword to slash at any infernal spirits, and went on to my girlfriend's smallholding.

I arrived practically gasping out my last breath, pale as a ghost, and with my groin swimming in sweat. My eyes were [wide and staring] as a corpse's, and I tell you, I'm not over the experience, even now.

Melissa grouched that I had taken my time, to arrive so tardily. She said 'If you had only come earlier you might have been some use to us. A wolf got in among the flock of the smallholding. He started draining the blood from the animals, expert as a butcher. He got away, but we got the last word. One of the slaves managed to put a spear through the beast's neck.'

* Perhaps this is why the werewolf's clothes could hang for a decade on an oak tree in Arcadia.

When I heard this I became wide awake and forgot all thoughts of rest. Instead, as soon as it was full daylight I ran off like the innkeeper who heard that his home had been robbed. When I reached the place where the clothes had turned to stone, they were gone, with nothing but bloodstains in their place.

Returning home [to the inn] I discovered my soldier already there, lying on his bed like a felled ox. The doctor was tending to a wound in his neck. I realized then that I had been in the company of a *versipellis*, though after that I'd not share a bite with him, even if you threatened me with death.[16]

THE MAGICAL MENAGERIE

Werewolves and vampires were far from being the only magical animals in the ancient world. Here we survey the other species, mainly with regard to their practical application to magic. This section is divided into two parts – animals in the ancient world with a magical connection, and animals that were themselves magical.

The magical menagerie is of great use to the apothecary who can harness the magical qualities of animals via their blood, teeth, bones and fur. Various magical concoctions make use of the body parts of birds – nineteen species of bird are known to have had magical properties – and mammals. Wolves, apes, weasels, mice, rats and horses (sometimes specifically foals, mares or stallions) are frequently mentioned in the magical papyri (see p. 46).

But be wary. Should the recipe for a spell include the tail feathers of a phoenix, you are best advised to look for an alternative. The 'Phoenix spell', which asks the god Osiris for a revelation, actually employs a type of purple-dyed paper called 'phoenix', relatively easily

Hyaena magic, my ass!

The most common animal used in Greek magical ingredients is, of all things, the donkey. The Romans favoured recipes based on the hyaena, presumably because this animal was suitably exotic. There are seventy-nine recorded uses of parts of the hyaena, mostly for medical magic – hyaena eyes could cure insanity, the liver could cure glaucoma and so on. Other popular animals were, in declining order of use, lizards, roosters, goats and the ibis.[17]

A magical pharmacy on legs: a Roman mosaic of a hyaena.

The apothecary's cheat sheet

Because people are so inquisitive, the names of herbs and other materials in inscriptions need translation. Without this precaution, people would not be prevented from practising magic through misunderstanding what they should use. These are [some] collected translations obtained from secret writings.

A snake's head	A leech
Ibis bone	Buckthorn [*Rhamnus cathartica*: the 'spell' in which this is used really does cure constipation, though it is too toxic to be safe for this purpose.]
Snake's blood	Haematite
Crocodile dung	Ethiopian soil
Lion semen	Human semen
Baboon hair	Dill seed
Blood of Hestia	Sandstone
Semen of Ares	Clover
Hyrax blood	Actual hyrax [sorry about that][18]

obtained today. This is just as well; there has only ever been one phoenix, and lately the species has become even rarer. Such code names in the magical papyri simultaneously make life simpler and more complicated for magic-users. Simpler because, as with 'phoenix paper', seemingly impossible-to-procure materials from exotic or magical beasts turn out not to be, but more complicated because the hopeful magician must work out whether an ingredient is the genuine article, or a disguised substitute.

THE MAGICAL CONNECTION
Cats

Cats have a major role in modern magic. They are the familiar of choice for witches both real (according to a given definition of 'real') and fictional. They can see the spirits of dead, and sense the use of magic. However, all these attributes have been awarded to the cat relatively recently. In the ancient world, cats were largely left to their own devices, not commonly kept as pets, or even as household animals. Rodent control in the ancient household was generally taken care of by weasels or pet snakes. Of the hundreds of spells known from the ancient world, cats appear only five times, while the weasel and the snake were both connected with magic, as we shall see.

This cat pilfering a larder in Pompeii gives a clue why they were not popular Roman pets.

Most people in the ancient world knew of the fanatical devotion given to cats in Egypt, where they were considered sacred. Killing an Egyptian cat, even by accident, earned the death penalty, according to the 1st-century BC Greek traveller Diodorus Siculus. The polytheistic ancients had no great wish to annoy the cat-goddess Bastet, even if she belonged to a different pantheon, and therefore cats were accorded a certain wary respect.

To the Romans, the cat symbolized liberty, since they reckoned of all animals the cat was the most free (as any cat-owner can attest). However, neither the Romans nor the Greeks seem to have considered them magical animals. The Greek gods each had an animal as their symbol. Athena famously had an owl, which for that reason remains a symbol of wisdom today. Zeus had an eagle, Hera a peacock, and so on. The cat too had a divine patron – but not, as we might expect, Hecate the witch goddess. Instead the cat was the beast of Artemis, the goddess of the hunt. She once transformed herself into a cat in an attempt to evade the uber-monster Typhon.

Weasels

When Hercules' mother was in labour the birth was prevented by the machinations of Hera, who was once again jealous because the philandering Zeus was the baby's father. The nurse recognized the problem, and used a subterfuge to bring about the hero's birth. This infuriated Hera, and in retaliation she turned the unfortunate nurse into a weasel. Hecate was one of the few goddesses who did not really care what Hera (or any other god) thought about her, and she had a soft spot for the underdog. Therefore she adopted the weasel/nurse as one of her familiars, and the weasel became her symbol thereafter. Thus, many households that adopted weasels did so in honour of the goddess, with the added benefit that their rodent problems magically disappeared.

The wrath of Hecate

They say the polecat was once a human. From what I have heard, she was called Gale. She was a sorceress and a dealer in spells. She was also both extremely unchaste and possessed of perverted sexual tastes. It has not escaped my attention that this is why the Goddess Hecate changed her into this diabolical creature.

Goddess, be good to me. Stories [about you] I shall leave for others to tell.[19]

Because of their association with Hecate, weasels were believed to have the ability to bring their dead pups back to life. Therefore, a dose of weasel meat, carefully salted and taken with the appropriate rituals, was believed to heal wounds and cure poisoning. One papyrus gives a spell that involves writing symbols on a triangular pot in weasel blood. Buried in the house of the victim, it would make him severely ill. (Perhaps fortunately, the magical symbols themselves are on a part of the papyrus too damaged to be legible.)

As domestic animals with a divine connection, weasels were studied by ancient scholars and magicians. The creature's actions, whether running between someone's feet or jumping on the table, could have prophetic significance. A weasel dragging a dead snake in its mouth presaged very bad news, because the snake was also magical. Sometimes demons might announce a future event through a weasel's call. So common were weasels, and so significant their connection to magic, that magical experts had to be well-versed in weasel lore in order to answer the questions of anxious householders.

Finally, given the connection with Hecate, we need not be surprised that some witches could change themselves into wereweasels. The ancient writer (and accused magician) Apuleius (AD 125–70) relates the story of a man charged with guarding a corpse so that witches could not remove body parts for magic before the man was buried.

(Having died suddenly, and not yet been ritually purified, the young corpse and organs were prime magical material.)

> Left alone with just a corpse for company! To keep up my spirits I sang to myself, and rubbed my eyes to sharpen them for duty. Twilight was followed by dark, and by the middle of the night I was more than somewhat scared. That was the point when a weasel suddenly slipped into the room. It reared up and fixed me with a piercing stare which was deeply alarming in a beast so small yet so bold.
>
> 'Shoo!' I yelled. 'Ungodly beast, get back to your rat companions. Get out before I give you something to remember me by. Leave!'
>
> As it turned and left the room, I felt myself sliding into a bottomless abyss of sleep, so deep that even Apollo could not have said which was the dead man – me or the actual corpse.[20]

The weasel, surely, bewitched him to fall into such deep slumber, which proved a problem – while our hero was literally sleeping like the dead, the witches who came in afterwards removed the ears and nose of the sleeper, believing him to be the corpse.

Snakes

Snakes have long been associated with medicine, for the snake is the symbolic animal of Asclepius, the god of healing. For centuries, the symbol of the medical profession has been the Rod of Asclepius – a snake twined about a staff. Except, that is, in the United States of America, where the symbol is two snakes around a staff with wings on top. This is an entirely different symbol – the *caduceus*, which is the staff of Hermes.

Above: The 'Hercules knot' in this Hellenistic armband contains a garnet. Both the knot and garnet symbolize faithfulness in marriage. The snake probably represents wisdom.

Below: Hygieia feeds the sacred snake curled around her father's staff.

Caduceus of Mercury with wings and twin snakes. More practical versions
of the staff had the snakes entwined only at the top, to form a handle.

Why medical practitioners in the USA adopted the symbol of mer-
chants and the god of hucksters and con-men (however appropriate
some cynics believe this adoption to be) is a matter of considerable
confusion and debate, but it seems generally accepted that the US
Army's medical corps is responsible. The *caduceus* shows a staff
parting two warring snakes, and the medical corps wanted to show
that they practised their craft between warring armies. From there,
the idea spread. Some defend the use of the *caduceus* symbol by US
doctors, pointing to medieval European medical texts that also use
it. This is probably inadvisable, because these older texts invoke

Hermes Trismegistus in his role as a magical being, and hark back to a time when magic and medicine were as intertwined as the snakes in the *caduceus*.

The *caduceus* controversy shows that while snakes have always had a role in healing, that role has not always been unambiguous – even today, in some parts of the world, the expression 'snake oil salesman' refers to someone who uses smooth talk to knowingly sell a dubious product. However, snakes are on firmer ground when it comes to prophecy.

As domestic animals, snakes were watched as closely as weasels to see what hints they might offer about the future.

> There is a story told that Tiberius Gracchus once found
> a pair of snakes in his bedroom. He consulted a seer, and
> was told he should on no account let both live. However, if
> he killed only the male snake, then he himself would die.
> If he killed the female, then [his wife] Cornelia would
> perish. Tiberius loved his wife deeply, and decided that
> he was an old man whereas his wife was relatively young.
> Therefore he released the female snake, killed the male,
> and died soon afterwards.[21]

Perhaps the most remarkable thing about this story is that snakes were so usual in Roman households that Tiberius was apparently equal to the challenging task of distinguishing a male from a female snake.

The prophetic snake *par excellence* was the python. This is because the original Python, a massive snake putting even its modern African equivalents to shame, was the guardian of the centre of the world, a place of huge oracular significance (see pp. 173–77). Python's downfall came about when Hera, in her usual congenial manner, compelled him to prevent the birth of the god Apollo because her husband Zeus

This Spartan cup shows a warrior battling a snake, perhaps Apollo taking on Python, or the hero Cadmus fighting a water-snake. Note the Medusa motif on the shield.

was the father, and she was not the mother. Though Python failed, a little-known fact about Apollo is that the god of art and music can be viciously vindictive. When grown to full godhood, Apollo sought out Python, killed him, and took over his oracle. Renamed the Delphic oracle, after the mountain sanctuary of Delphi where it was based, this site became the premier oracular consultancy in the ancient world. The priestess who delivered the oracles was still called the Pythia, or 'pythoness'.

'Bad' snakes came from bad people, as this text explains:

They say that the putrefying marrow of a dead man
turns into a snake....These evil creatures are created
from the spines of evil men, after the manner of their

lives....The corpse of a wrong-doer earns the punishment for his misdeeds by giving rise to a snake.[22]

Another serpentine sub-species of note is the basilisk. While this creature is not known in the wild today, ancient writers treated it as a consummately deadly but otherwise natural species. *Basilici serpentis* (to give the beast its taxonomic name) was a North African snake only 30 cm (12 in.) long. The name 'basilisk' is derived from the Greek word for 'king', and refers to the white, diadem-shaped marking on the snake's head. While notorious for being able to kill with the power of its gaze, basilisks were also incredibly venomous. This would be very useful to brewers of *pharmaka*, if only there was some way of safely handling the poison; an anecdote offered by Pliny illustrates the problem:

It is believed that once a man on a horse stabbed one with a spear. The venom travelled up through the spear and killed both the man and the horse he was riding.[23]

A basilisk gambols in this corner of a 2nd-century AD Roman mosaic.

Yet even this incredibly deadly animal (using the word 'incredible' in its proper sense of 'hard to believe') had its kryptonite. Weasels were immune to the worst a basilisk could do, and their bite was immediately fatal to the snake. The association between this story and the entirely natural rivalry of the cobra and mongoose suggests an Indian origin for at least part of the basilisk legend.

Dogs

Today the humble mutt is regarded as a thoroughly mundane animal. Yet in antiquity it was a dog that Hecate took as a familiar alongside the weasel. This particular dog was Hecuba, queen of Troy, magically transformed into a large black dog (see p. 100). While dogs today are generally considered unmagical, the Hecate connection has ensured

This is one of two mosaics warning '*cave canem*' ('beware of the dog') unearthed in Pompeii, a testament to the ubiquity of dogs in Roman life.

an exception for black dogs, especially mysterious large black dogs that turn up unexpectedly. In most European countries this is said to presage a death.

Being magical was certainly not an asset to ancient dogs, as they were frequently sacrificed as suitable messengers to the gods. In one particularly gruesome ceremony on 3 August every year the Romans actually crucified dogs as part of a fertility rite.

Most ancient sacrifices were of animals deemed culturally acceptable to eat, because an ancient bargain specifies that of a sacrificed animal's physical remains the gods get the hide and the bones, while the humans get the meat. But the Greeks and Romans did not eat dogs. Dog sacrifices were therefore usually limited to offerings to the gods of the Underworld, for in such sacrifices the entire body of the victim was consumed by fire. Besides, Hecate liked getting dogs. When she walked abroad on moonless nights, domestic dogs would howl. They were answered by the ghostly canine retinue that accompanied the goddess, while sensible humans burrowed deep under their bedcovers.

Like modern cats, dogs could see ghosts and demons. A dog barking at nothing was assumed to have seen one or the other. Dog parts appear frequently in magic concoctions, a role reprised in Shakespeare's *Macbeth*, as witches devoted to Hecate brew up a potion including 'Eye of newt, and toe of frog/Wool of bat, and tongue of dog'.[24] While such conjurations are considered abhorrent today, those suffering from a cold or rheumatism might like to experiment with the ancient remedy of being gently rubbed down with a puppy.

MAGICAL SPECIES

These creatures are purely magical, and encountered extremely rarely (to those with magical abilities) or not at all (for the rest of the world). Since some of the more powerful spells require parts from these beasts, what follows is a quick description and a summary of where these creatures are least unlikely to be found.

The griffin

Griffins were found in Scythia, or the mountainous regions north of the Black Sea. While our best description of this animal comes from Aelian, a 2nd-century AD Greek writer, griffins have been around much longer than that – similar, but even more ancient, descriptions are known from the Middle East.

> They are wolf-sized, and enormously strong. They are winged like birds, though four-footed. Their legs and claws resemble those of a lion. The body is black, but the chest feathers are red. The wings themselves are white.[25]

We are told that these birds were poor flyers, but physically powerful – Philostratus quotes the Indian sage Larkhas, who claimed that having wings allowed griffins to overpower elephants, especially as the griffins were 'as strong as lions'.[26] Those needing strength often adopted the griffin as a symbol, and so the griffin was a common motif on the shields of hoplite warriors. Amulets intended to boost the strength, power or resolve of an individual might also feature this mighty creature.

Two things make the griffin particularly interesting (see box for the second). The first is that the creature combines elements of the lion with those of the eagle. (The later medieval and heraldic showing the

Were griffins real?

Modern science is slowly coming to the conclusion that griffins –
or animals rather like them – might actually have existed:

> Here we describe a new basal neornithischian dinosaur from the
> Jurassic of Siberia with small scales around the distal hind-limb,
> larger imbricated scales around the tail, monofilaments around
> the head and the thorax, and more complex featherlike structures
> around the humerus, the femur, and the tibia.[27]

In other words, in the Jurassic era there was a griffin-sized, four-
legged feathered species that was evolving wings. Herodotus also reports
having seen the skeletons of creatures that the Egyptians called 'winged
snakes', which 'had wings closely resembling those of bats'.[28] How people
living three thousand years ago might have known of such creatures
is open to speculation.

The noble griffin in a 17th-century European woodcut.

creature as a chimera with the fore-body of an eagle and the hind parts
of a lion are simplifications of the ancient descriptions.) The eagle
represented Zeus and his Roman aspect of Jupiter, which is why the
Roman legions marched to war under the symbol of the eagle, while
the lion represented the Anatolian mother-goddess Cybele. Thus an
animal with attributes of an eagle and a lion combined the strongest
features of the masculine and feminine elements.

Harpies

These beings are less a species than a family. They numbered less
than a dozen and lived in the area of the Black Sea, just south of
the griffin's natural habitat. Ancient writers depicted the harpies as
an ugly mixture of crow and human. An anonymous author known
as Pseudo-Hyginus offers this unflattering description: 'Feathered,
heads like cocks, and both wings and human arms. The human parts
are female as they have breasts and bellies as well as large claws'.[29]

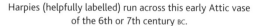

Harpies (helpfully labelled) run across this early Attic vase
of the 6th or 7th century BC.

It is probable that the harpies are personifications of the storm winds that their sudden, violent attacks resembled. They flew faster than birds, and were responsible for sudden, otherwise inexplicable abductions. For example, Homer tells us that the 'daughters of Pandareus' were seized by the harpies and carried off just before their wedding day.[30]

Occasionally there are references to the harpies being used as a magical form of transport faster than anything otherwise known in the ancient world. 'Let the Harpies snatch me up, and carry me over the sea to Lolkos', says Apollonius Rhodius.[31] Since the harpies were commanded by the god Aeolus, lord of the winds, it may have been possible for a magic-user to make such a bargain, dangerous though it would be.

Note that the harpies are a species related to, but distinct from the bird-woman sirens who were killed off after an encounter with Odysseus.[32] Death was not the end for these creatures, who became the handmaidens of Persephone, queen of the Underworld. While still in the world, the sirens drove men mad with the beauty of their song. These days, their mechanical descendants remain creatures of ill-omen, though they sound far less sweet from their perches atop police cars and ambulances.

Dragons

Like the griffin, the dragon is a purely magical animal, the power of which is more inspirational than practical. Magical spells do not usually feature dragon parts, not only because dragons are both scarce and far away, but also because of the extreme difficulty involved in separating the rest of the dragon from the requisite bits.

The reputed power and ferocity of the dragon caused it to be adopted as a symbol of the legions of later Rome. The 'draco' is assumed to have been a cloth tube that filled out in the wind. The first

The dragons of Medea

It took a ferocious and powerful woman to master such powerful beasts as dragons – who else but Medea:

> For nine days and nine nights she roamed the earth [collecting herbs], carried by her team of harnessed dragons. Then she came back. The only thing that had affected the dragons was the odour of those herbs, which caused them to shed the ancient skins that they had worn for so many years.[33]

Medea makes another getaway, this time on a chariot pulled by dragons.

A concerned Athena (note the griffin on her helmet) watches as the Colchian Dragon swallows Jason. Medea later persuaded the dragon to disgorge the hero.

appearance of this symbolic animal on the battlefield can still be viewed today on Trajan's column, where it inspired Dacian warriors against the Roman soldiers who later adopted it.

While dragons have been reported from areas as diverse as Wales and China, the species known to antiquity was *Drakon Indikos*, the Indian Dragon. Some of these beasts reached a great size, with one of the largest reported as being 140 cubits, or around 64 metres (70 yards), from tooth to tail. This dragon was allegedly owned by an Indian king at the time of Alexander the Great, who made strenuous, but ultimately unsuccessful, efforts to see the beast.

Dragons have been described by various authors in antiquity, starting with Homer around 800 BC[34] all the way to Aelian in the 2nd century AD. Philostratus gives perhaps the best description,

Bilbo Gyges

Both Plato and Herodotus described the adventures of a certain Gyges.
He, while exploring in some caves under a mountain, came across a ring
of the type described by Philostratus, set with the stones from a dragon's
skull. Gyges discovered that if he slipped this ring upon his finger and
twisted it, he became invisible. Any resemblance to a certain hobbit
who discovered a ring under similar circumstances with a similar result
is presumably coincidental.

and divides the species into three sub-types – the marsh dragon
(a relatively small specimen), the plains dragon (around the size of
a wild boar), and the mountain dragon, which grows to great size.
Philostratus hints that there was a magical use for the plains dragons:

> They are red, and when mature they have serrated backs,
> while their scales shine as though made of silver. This kind
> carry their heads high, and have a type of beard. The pupils
> of their eyes are a fiery stone, and this is said to have
> unnatural powers. This is employed for secret purposes.[35]

The mountain dragon was also hunted by the native peoples,
'For they say that in their heads there are stones coloured like flowers,
flashing in many shades. If set into rings these possess mystical
powers'.[36]

Anyone seeking a repository of immense magical power is advised
to head for India and there locate the lost city of Parax. Built within
a hollowed-out mountain, this was a city of immense size. The men
were trained as dragon-hunters from childhood, and collected a
massive stockpile of dragon's heads, which is stored right in the
centre of the hidden city.

The phoenix

A mural in a Pompeian tavern bears the motto *'Phoenix felix: et tu'* – 'Fortunate is the Phoenix – and you!'

> There is a sacred bird called the Phoenix. I have never seen it, except in pictures, because it is exceptionally rare, even in Egypt. According to the people of [the sacred city of] Heliopolis it only turns up every five hundred years....
>
> It seems barely credible to me, but this is what they relate that the bird does. He flies all the way over from Arabia, and carries with him the myrrh-coated corpse of his parent. This he buries at the Temple of the Sun.[37]

The fortunate Phoenix found in the Taverna of Euxinus in Pompeii.

Herodotus claimed to have seen pictures, allegedly painted from life, showing the phoenix to be a bird the size of an eagle with vivid red and gold plumage. This description is supported by Pliny the Elder.

> There is only one in the whole world, so it is not seen very often. The bird is the size of an eagle, mostly purple in colour, but with brilliant golden feathers around the neck. On the other hand, the tail is bright blue with long pinkish feathers intermingled. There is a crest on the chest, and a feathery tuft on the head.
>
> The senator and famous scholar Manilius was the first Roman to describe the bird, and he did so with great precision....It lives 540 years, and when it is old it builds a nest from cassia [a spicy evergreen] and twigs of incense. It fills the nest with perfumed plants and lies upon these to die.
>
> From the marrow of the bones comes a kind of little worm which develops into a young bird. The first thing this bird does is to perform the funeral rites for its predecessor, and it carries the entire nest to Heliopolis where it deposits it upon the altar of the Sun.[38]

That the phoenix arises from the ashes of itself appears to have been a later conflation with another sacred Egyptian bird called the *bennu*. However, once the image of the bird arising from its own immolation became established, the obvious connection was made with the nascent Christian religion. Thereafter the phoenix became a symbol of rebirth and renewal.

This symbolism was sometimes seen on ancient amulets and has been adopted with enthusiasm by a number of modern insurance companies. During the late 19th century, American pioneers began building a settlement near ruins left by the native Hohokam peoples

'You must be ready to burn yourself in your own flame.
How could you rise anew if you have not first become ashes?'
Nietzsche, *Thus Spake Zarathustra*.

in Arizona. The rebirth of a new city from ancient ruins inspired a classically minded citizen to suggest the name of Phoenix for the place, which is now the state capital with a population of over a million.

CHAPTER FIVE

Προστασία από τις κακές τέχνες

PROTECTION AGAINST THE ARTS
OF DARKNESS

Phylactery Charm: Take a sheet of hieratic papyrus
or a thin sheet of gold or silver.* Inscribe as follows:

KMEPHIS CHPHYRIS IAEO IAO OO
AIONIAEORAPHRENE....

After these names, draw a figure as follows – the snake
biting its tail [the Ouroboros snake] with the names written
inside the circle thus formed. Add the set of symbols....

This is accompanied by the incantation 'Protect the body
and entire soul of me; [insert name here]'. When the charm
has been consecrated wear it. It is a protection against
demons, ghosts and [magically induced] sickness and
suffering.[1]

Life in the ancient world was a chancy business. A perfectly healthy
youth could sicken and die painfully within a few days, or an older
individual might drop dead with no warning at all – Julius Caesar's
father bent down one day to pull on his boots, and never got up again.

The human mind is seldom prepared to believe that such things
'just happen'. If someone dies unexpectedly, there must be a reason
for it. In a world that knew little about burst appendixes or massive
heart attacks, there was a simple explanation: dark magic.

* If you are penniless and desperate, use tin.

Ouroboros, the tail-eating snake, encompasses the god Serapis,
who is enthroned above a crocodile.

Once the cause had been decided, inquiring minds set out to discover exactly how that magic worked. It depended entirely on the individual whether the motives behind such research were noble – working out the mechanics of dark spells to determine how they should be warded off – or more sinister. Innocent people needed to know what vicious and depraved spells to defend against; but inevitably some people rather fancied using such spells themselves.

As well as what we might call 'targeted magic' (such as the curses and *agonistic* spells that we met in Chapter 3), there existed random nastiness of a magical kind that was less discriminating in its choice of victim. Just as one could be hurt by a runaway cart or bitten by a rabid dog, being in the wrong place at the wrong time could make you the victim of unfriendly magical forces. These forces needed to be warded off, just as one needed to take precautions against plague, robbers or savage animals. For this reason there existed a minor industry in counter-spells and amulets that deflected dark magic. Keeping the home free of unfriendly magical influences was a regular part of household routine.

DAYS OF THE RESTLESS DEAD

An experiment by the 20th-century behavioural psychologist B. F. Skinner has shown that it is possible to induce superstition in pigeons.[2] This is because animals are designed to detect patterns, and this is especially true of the human animal. Once a pattern has been established, confirmation bias does the rest. If you believe Friday the thirteenth is unlucky, then on that day you are more likely to notice minor misfortunes that you would ignore on any other day. This superstition-influenced observation confirms your superstition, and in turn makes you even more certain that every Friday falling on the thirteenth is unlucky.

The Romans took note of the days on which their armies had lost significant battles and declared them *dies nefasti*, 'days of ill omen', on which no public business could be conducted. The 'Ides' (the thirteenth or the fifteenth day of the month) were also *nefasti*. Therefore the assassins should have known that the Ides of March were not a good time to, for example, kill Julius Caesar. Indeed, the enterprise turned out badly, and not just for the victim – in the civil wars that followed the murder, most of the assassins were dead within a decade. The days that came after the Ides were also considered somewhat risky.

There were widely observed *dies atri*, or unlucky days. On such days one never started a project, and took care to not even mention the name of Janus, the God of Beginnings. Because of the risk of

Symbols of freedom: this coin, issued by the assassins of Julius Caesar,
shows the cap worn by newly freed Roman slaves, between two daggers.

starting a pregnancy, sex was a risky proposition. Getting married
or starting a long journey was totally out of the question. Those suffering unhappy marriages might like to check if their anniversaries
fall on 24 June, 5 October, or 8 November. The Romans believed that
the gates of the Underworld were open at those times and all sorts
of malevolent spirits were abroad. For the same reason, no Roman
general fought a battle on those days if he could possibly avoid it.

In fact, if you wanted a happy marriage, it was best to avoid
May altogether. 'Bad women get married in May', observed the poet
Ovid, adding:

Our ancestors shut the temple doors on those days
And closed they remain today,
In this season sacred to the dead.
Widow or maid, this is no time to marry
She who marries then, will not live long thereafter.[3]

May was perhaps the most unfortunate month of the year. Some Roman etymologists reckoned that 'May' comes from *Maiores,* the Latin for 'ancestors', for this was the month when the dead were honoured. May started out well with the *Floralia*, a rite of spring involving drunkenness, nudity and general debauchery, but after the *nundinae* – the first market day of the month – things took a darker turn.

The worst days were the ninth, eleventh and thirteenth. So unlucky were these days that the Romans went on the offensive and launched an all-out assault on unwanted ghostly spirits in a set of rituals collectively known as the Lemuria. In the Lemuria, 'good' household spirits were encouraged to protect the home and those within, while wandering ghosts were gently urged off the premises. Alongside these lost and confused souls were malevolent spirits trying to infiltrate the household to cause mischief.

The cleansing ritual began at the sixth hour of the night of the ninth day of May. The 'man of the house' kicked off the proceedings by three times washing his hands in pure water in front of the Lares (images of the household's guardian spirits). He wore a tunic without

---

Lost spirits

Especially in need of shooing were those souls that had died without being given a proper burial and were now searching, rather like stray cats, for a household they could attach themselves to.

> We also call 'demon' those human *anima* [spirits] which have departed the body at the end of life....Now some of these fall properly into the care of their descendants and we call them Lares ('household gods', though here the appellation 'gods' is only honorific). But other spirits...are in a sort of exile, denied a home and wandering without direction.[4]

Ancient home insurance – two Lares and a snake in a mural from Pompeii.

knots, hooks or any ties to which a spirit might attach itself. Since it is hard to wear footwear without any of these things, he was barefoot.

He had a mouthful of beans (beans were a somewhat supernatural legume), which he spat into places where the unwanted spirits (*lemures*) might be lurking. The reason for spitting was because he needed his hands free to make the symbol of the *ficus* – thumb thrust between the second and third fingers of a clenched fist. This gesture evoked the fertility of the Great Goddess, the Magna Mater (her clitoris, to be precise), and it had the same effect on *lemures* as a crucifix would later have on vampires.

The beans were a sort of ransom paid to the *lemures*, and now those spirits had been brought forth, the rest of the household banged on pots and pans to make them feel that there must be more relaxing places to haunt. Anyone in the group who had the urge to howl like a wolf was encouraged to do so, to add to the generally unwelcoming atmosphere.

After every floor in the house had been covered by the exorcizing party (the really conscientious did this nine times, nine being three times three) the next thing was to clean the house from top to bottom, thus ousting any spirits from nooks and crannies to which they had become attached. This part of the ritual is still a good idea for other reasons, which is why today 'spring cleaning' remains something of a household tradition in the northern hemisphere.

If the ghosts happened to have a particular interest in the household, then expulsion became a lot harder. For example, the emperor Nero had a problem with being haunted by his mother. 'He got to the point of summoning mages, and had them perform a rite to summon her spirit so that he could attempt to cool her anger'. So says the biographer Suetonius,[5] who does not make the obvious point that the easiest way to avoid being haunted by your mother is not to execute her in the first place.

While honest souls were giving the house a good purge of unwelcome dust and phantasms, witches and other magic-users preferred to spend the Lemuria in graveyards and at crossroads in the hope of recruiting these same restless spirits for their own nefarious purposes.

EXORCISM

The restless dead did not confine their search for a home to houses. Sometimes they took up residence in people. Since this was an anti-social act by any standard of conduct, such spirits were negatively defined as *necrodemonia*, which made them liable for expulsion by any means possible. It was generally agreed that Jewish exorcists were best suited for the task, possibly because the exclusive nature of their god made their faith less welcoming to other supernatural beings than the 'come one, come all' attitude of polytheism.

> I myself have seen Eleazar, a man of my tribe, in the presence of [the emperor] Vespasian, expelling the spirits of demons from the bodies of men. This was done before his sons, his officers and many other soldiers.
> He performed the cure thus. First he put a ring to the nose of the possessed. Under the seal of the ring was a root prepared according to the prescriptions of Solomon. Caught by the smell, the demon was drawn by Eleazar down through the nostrils. When it emerged, the victim would promptly collapse.[6]

At this point, or just before, the exorcist would address the demon directly. Discovering the name of the spirit was important, since this would help to determine the nature of the possession – whether by a demon, a dispossessed spirit, or a vengeful one. Once the type of spirit was known, more precise rites could be performed to prevent repossession of the body by the same spirit in the future.

We see the same importance of smell plus knowledge of the name of a possessing spirit in a short spell in the magical papyri. 'If you say the name of the demon to a man possessed, while holding sulphur and bitumen to his nose, the demon will cry out and depart'.[7] But a simple departure was not enough for Eleazar, who liked to finish with a flourish:

> To demonstrate the power that he controlled, he would set a cup or a bowl a few paces away. This was filled with water. As the spirit fled the body, he would command it to overturn the vessel. When this happened, those watching knew that the spirit had truly gone.[8]

Assyrian origins

The Assyrians believed that all illnesses were the result of evil taking possession of a person's body, and developed a variety of rituals and exorcisms to cleanse the affliction. One clay tablet describing an exorcism, found by archaeologists in the famous Library of Ashurbanipal (king of Assyria from 668–627 BC) in the ancient city of Nineveh, begins with these ominous words:

> The evil curse like a demon fixes on a man
> A raging voice over him is fixed
> The evil curse is a great calamity
> That man the evil curse slaughters like a lamb
> His god from over him departs
> His goddess stands angry at his side
> The raging voice like a cloak covers him and bears him away...[9]

Exorcism tablets.

Demons, lost spirits and hostile ghosts were far from the only problems. Defenders against dark forces also had to worry about their fellow humans.

THE 'EVIL EYE'

The phenomenon of the 'Evil Eye' appears often in discussions of superstition and magic in the classical world, although it is not entirely clear what the Evil Eye actually was. It seems to revolve around the idea that the gaze of a malicious individual can cause harm, but the phrase 'Evil Eye' is modern. Neither the Greeks nor the Romans used it, partly because they did not distinguish evil as an abstract quality separate from wrongdoing, whereas in modern terms something can be considered 'evil' without actually doing anything bad (you just know it will get around to it eventually).

Yet the ancients certainly believed in the concept behind the Evil Eye, and being of an analytical disposition, they attempted to categorize what they were talking about. One of the best ancient discussions of the topic is found in the *Moralia* of the biographer, priest and philosopher Plutarch, who recorded a dialogue with one of his colleagues, Megistes. When Megistes observes that 'it can happen that people are injured just by a look', and queries just how that might be so, Plutarch responds:

> Since no one can dispute that men are affected by what
> they see, why should it not be also true that they affect
> what they look upon? Does not the glance of someone
> beautiful quickly rouse to flame the passion of the one
> so regarded?....Does not the soul when affected work upon
> the body? Sorrow, fear and anger change our complexions,
> and envy so deforms the soul that it fills the body with bile.

And when the envious person fixes his eyes on another, can not the person he sees draw out that venom? In this way he who is looked upon is hurt.

His colleague, Gaius, echoes this view:

Philosophers reckon that the envious project a force which is imbued with the disturbing and poisonous traits of the person from whom they come, and these injure the person so observed both in body and mind.[10]

Of course, we in the modern era do not believe that it is possible to poison by a look, but phrases such as 'if looks could kill' and 'looking daggers' show that we clearly still understand the underlying idea.

The 'Evil Eye' in a house in Antioch, Syria. The inscription reads '[Your look is reflected] back at you'.

A *fascinus* with bells was called a *tintinnabulum*.
This well-endowed specimen is from Pompeii.

Today certain people are referred to as 'toxic' characters, as though their very presence poisons the atmosphere around them. The Greeks and Romans simply took these concepts more literally.

The amulet that best deflected the Evil Eye was the *fascinus* (the casting of malevolent incantations was described by the Latin verb 'fascinare', from which we get the English word 'fascinate'). To see what a *fascinus* looks like, half of the human race need merely look downwards next time they are naked. That the *fascinus* is an accurate depiction of a penis is unsurprising. The Romans considered this organ to be the prime source of health and fertility, so it was naturally the body part most likely to be injured by the glare of a jealous individual. An artificial phallus, prepared with the necessary charms to make it appear (to the malignant force of the Evil Eye) more realistic than the real thing acted as a sort of psychic lightning rod, attracting and absorbing the worst of the impact of an envious gaze.

Partly as a result of this, and partly because the Romans considered the phallus a symbol of natural bounty, depictions of male genitalia crop up in Roman society in what we would today consider to be highly inappropriate settings. For example, jewelry with the *fascinus* of a size that would only be suitable for a very young girl has been discovered. (Having no natural competition, so to speak, the *fascinus* was even more effective when carried by females.) On the opposite end of the spectrum, gigantic phalluses requiring several men to hold them up would joyfully be displayed in parades. Other phalluses appeared as decorations on lamps or, ornamented with bells, as wind chimes.

The Romans had a god for pretty much everything, so it was inevitable that the tutelary deity of the phallus should be the god Fascinus. This deity was often linked in Roman minds with Bacchus and Priapus, though by some reckonings his cult dated back to the founding of the city. As well as protecting children (for children were often envied by the childless), Fascinus extended his reach all the way up through society to that most envied of all Romans, the conquering general.

> Fascinus protects not only infants, but generals also....
> A *fascinus* is attached underneath the chariot of the
> victorious general in a Roman Triumph. It is there like an
> attending doctor, to guard against the effects of envy.[11]

Fascinus did not have his own temple. Instead, the Romans somehow decided that a divine entity taking the form of the male sex organ should best be kept in the care of the Vestal Virgins.

While amulets were useful protections against malevolent incantations, Romans took a variety of other precautions as a matter of

Magical Egyptian amulet of the Byzantine era, designed to help menstruating women. It is carved of haematite, which was believed to stop the flow of blood.

routine. For example, after eating a boiled egg or a snail, it was customary to smash the shell. With the breaking, any malevolent spells in the vicinity would assume that their destructive work was done. In extreme cases smashing a pot could have the same effect, and even more powerfully. Echoes of this concept survive today: after the making of an especially solemn toast, the glass is traditionally broken.

Another counter-magical remedy available to citizens of the classical world was simply to take the perpetrator to court. Greeks and Romans of all levels of society were fully convinced that the dark arts were on occasion actively employed by malefactors, and legislators were among the believers. They also believed that, while amulets and counter-spells were all very well, nothing had the stopping power of a legal injunction formally issued by a magistrate.

One of Rome's oldest law codes was the Twelve Tables, officially established in the 5th century BC. Table Eight forbids the chanting

---

The breaking and entering spell

Take the navel of a male crocodile, the egg of a scarab beetle, and the heart of a baboon. Put these into an aquamarine faïence container. Then to open a door just bring the container to the lock and say:

'By Thaim Tholach Thembaor Theagon Pentatheschi Boeti; you who possesses the power of the depths, give that to me that the way might be open for me. For I say to you Sauamboch Mera Cheozaph Ossala Bymbel Pouo Toutho Oirerei Arnoch.'[12]

Alternatively, use a key.

---

of *malum carmen* (malevolent spells), and also the use of magic to charm crops from one man's fields to another – a serious issue when most people's livelihood came from agriculture. The obvious potential for misuse of this law was demonstrated in a case described by the elder Pliny.[13] A man with a smallholding was prosecuted by neighbours envious of his abundant harvests. The prosecution argued that the only way the accused's fields could have been so fertile was through magic that charmed away the produce from adjoining fields. Before the jury took their vote, the smallholder demonstrated that his magical prowess consisted of well-kept tools, trained workers, and the judicious use of fertilizer. The charge was dismissed, but the case shows that prosecution was a potent weapon in the armoury of counter-measures against illicit magics.

In the 1st century BC, the dictator Sulla decided that the current legislation was too wishy-washy. Though he himself was rather inclined to divination and seeking favour from the gods, actual magicians needed adding to his already very long list of victims. Sulla laid down the law in no uncertain terms:

Those who know magic should be thrown to the beasts [in the arena] or crucified. Any actual magicians should be burned alive. Books of magic should not be kept in a household. If any such books are discovered, the books should be publicly burned and the rest of the property confiscated. The owners should be exiled to an island if they are upper-class, and otherwise executed.

It is forbidden to even know magic, let alone practise it as a craft or trade. If someone is given a *pharmaka* for medical reasons and dies from the treatment, the giver is to be exiled to an island if upper-class and executed if not.[14]

Clearly, if you were a magician, you had better be an aristocratic magician.

We get an interesting commentary on this law from the *Digest of Justinian*, compiled half a millennium later.[15] While happy with the general disposal of magicians, it seems that later lawyers were careful to distinguish between concoctions designed for the health and welfare of the patient and those specifically prepared to kill him. The law also specified that it fell to the person preparing the drug to ensure that the potion was not harmful, and that legal remedies were available if the drug did have an adverse effect.

While these prohibitions have made it impossible for later ages to obtain any Roman manuals on witchcraft, there is a mass of contemporary evidence that demonstrates that the Romans, like the Greeks, generally ignored the commands of the authorities. They continued to seek out witches and sorcerers and paid them well for their services, both for magic and counter-magic.

Amulets, being defensive in nature, were not included in the general proscription of magic. Therefore, a number of formulas for the making of amulets have been preserved, and in some cases the amulets themselves. An interesting example was discovered recently in Romania, inscribed with magical signs and a crude drawing, which appears to represent the demon that the spell addresses. The amulet was evidently designed not to absorb a spell, as did *fascini*, but to deflect it, for the inscription reads:

> Demon who hangs over me in this place, go!
> Haunt instead Julia Cyrilla's house
> Do this for me. Now, now, now![16]

We also see amulets being used for healing purposes, though it is usually unclear whether the amulet was designed to heal the sufferer, or to act against the malign spirit or spell causing the problem. Probably both solutions were attempted, for belief in the healing powers of certain minerals and crystals is certainly enduring. In Roman times, haematite was regarded as useful against pain in the liver. Haematite bracelets intended to prevent tiredness and keep the wearer energetic and free from arthritis have been discovered on Amazon.com listings in AD 2018.

Not everyone was convinced. When the great Athenian politician Pericles (494–429 BC) was sick, he drew the attention of visiting friends to an amulet that the women of the household had put around his neck 'with the implication that he was in remarkably poor shape if he allowed himself to suffer such idiocy.'[17]

CHARM TO PROTECT A MAGICAL PRACTITIONER WHILE PERFORMING RITES

Finally, having gone to some length to describe the perils of using magic, it would be remiss not to offer the hopeful magic-user some form of protection while practising the art.

As you perform a conjuration, wear this [amulet] strung on a thong made of donkey-skin. The amulet should be of rolled silver, and with a bronze stylus the name of a hundred letters* should be inscribed.

ACHCHORACH
ACHACHPTOU
MICHACHCH
OCHARACHO
CHCAPATOU
MECHORASH
ARACHOCHAP
TOUMIMECHO
CHAPTOUCHA
RACHPTOUCH
ACHCHOCHAR
ACHOPTENAC
HOCHEU[18]

* The inscription is actually 126 letters, because of internal repetitions. What it once meant is anyone's guess.

Κεί σερα, σερα

LOOKING TO THE FUTURE

> Now I am aware of no people, however refined and
> learned or however savage and ignorant, which does
> not think that signs are given of future events, and that
> certain persons can recognize those signs and foretell
> events before they occur.[1]

In the past it was easier to tell the future. This is because for the ancients, the future was as unchangeable as the past. What would be, would be. This is not to deny the existence of free will; it was just that people freely took the path leading to their preordained future. Humans can choose, but fate knows what their choice will be.

In Greek myth, the story of Oedipus illustrates this well. The child who was destined to kill his father and marry his mother would not have done any of those things were it not for the extreme measures that everyone voluntarily took to prevent it from happening. On learning the prophecy, the father ordered his baby son to be abandoned on a hillside. Instead, the baby was adopted by the king of Corinth. Unaware of who his real father was, Oedipus met and killed him in a quarrel. Later he married the widow. Had he known his true father from the start, Oedipus would probably have enjoyed a peaceful life – but there is no escape from destiny.

While a modern mechanical Nostradamus has to examine a multitude of probable futures to predict what is to come, the ancients worked with just one fixed future. This made things easier. If there

The fable of Death and the wizard

It is not known when this fable was first told, though it is undoubtedly ancient. The basic theme is the same as the story of Oedipus – the more people struggle to avoid the inevitable, the more they work toward making it happen.

A wizard of Damascus was in the market one day when a fellow died in a sudden accident. The wizard saw the incident, and being magical, he also saw Death come to claim the victim. Just before he did so, Death stopped and gave the wizard a long, calculating stare.

The wizard correctly realized that this interest on the part of Death signalled his own impending demise, and he panicked. He hired the fastest horse he could find, and almost killed the animal in a mad dash to get away. Riding non-stop for a day and a night, he eventually reached Antioch, where he collapsed and died from exhaustion.

When he saw that Death had come to claim him, the wizard said, 'I have been expecting you ever since I saw that look you gave me in Damascus.'

'Actually', confessed Death, 'That look was just confusion. I didn't know how you could be in Damascus, when I knew that I was meeting you today in Antioch.'

Ironically, this story is now a paradigm used in predictive models by machine intelligence.[2]

was only one future that was going to happen, no matter what, then the only issue – albeit a big issue – was how to see it. Though difficult, the task was far from impossible. This is because although humans experience time as a sequence of events, the ancients believed that ex-humans (the spirits of the dead) and most divine beings instead saw time as a sort of large and complete flow-chart, on which the present was a moving dot.

Therefore, one way for a human to gain foreknowledge of the future was to talk to someone outside time who already knew that future. As we have seen, there are a variety of ways of getting in touch with such entities (though persuading these entities to be helpful presents an additional challenge). A second means was – and is – to get in touch with a living person with a talent for seeing ahead. The problem with this approach is that the only way of sorting out the fakers and charlatans from the real thing is to see if the predictions come true, and by then it is generally too late.

The third way was to cultivate such a talent yourself. For the ancients all the universe was a single, connected holistic entity. Today, a flurry of activity on social media and a liquor store preparing a large order are precursor events that lead inevitably to a party at Bill's house that evening. In the same way, in ancient times, the movement of Mars into the house of Aries, combined with a flight of cranes going northwest to southeast meant that Licinia's child would be a baby boy. Everything was connected. The issue was how to join the dots.

The ancients developed a variety of means to predict the future, but note that while astrology is discussed here to some degree, the subject is as much modern magic (or 'science' to its many believers) as it is ancient magic. Although the methods of prediction have remained largely unchanged through the millennia, astrology is a thoroughly modern affair. When Instagram and Snapchat offer to send daily horoscopes to users' smartphones, 'ancient magic' does not properly describe the topic.

The twelve astrological houses and their relationship to the planets and Olympian gods are so well known that almost every person in the modern West knows their birth sign and associated character traits. ('I don't believe in astrology, because we Scorpios are natural sceptics.') The only major significant difference was that the ancients paid as much attention to the sign in the ascendant at their birth as they did to their sun sign. Thus the emperor Augustus, born in mid-September 63 BC, was by modern standards a Virgo, his sun sign, but he adopted as his symbol the Capricorn, his ascendant sign.

Above: Gaia, with her four children (the seasons), reclines while Aeon, the god of eternity, stands in the sphere of the heavens encircled by the houses of the zodiac.

Below: The emperor Augustus adopted the Capricorn as his personal symbol. It also became the symbol of his favourite legion, Legio II Augusta.

It is your destiny, young Augustus

The emperor Augustus started life in an aristocratic, but relatively undistinguished, family. One of the first indications of his future greatness allegedly came from a consultation with an astrologer. (Though cynical historians point out that Augustus was *very* good at propaganda, and this story seems to have become public only after he became emperor.)

> While [young men] at Apollonia, Augustus and Agrippa went up to the consultancy of Theogenes the astrologer. Agrippa was the first to try his fortune, and it was predicted to be almost unimaginably great and felicitous. Out of fear that his own fate was something lesser, Augustus persistently tried to conceal his birth date. After repeated requests, he gave it, unwillingly and hesitantly.
>
> [On doing the reading] Theogenes threw himself at Augustus' feet [as to the master of the world]. Thereafter Augustus had such faith in the destiny revealed by his horoscope that he made it public, and even issued a silver coin bearing the sign of Capricorn, the constellation beneath which he was born.[3]

Those with an interest in this ancient but also very modern form of divination have an abundance of texts to choose from, most of which are directly or indirectly based on the *Tetrabiblos* of Claudius Ptolemy. This masterwork on the subject was written in AD 170, and has been regularly published ever since. Readers are recommended to the English translation by Frank Egleston Robbins in the *Loeb Classical Library*, which has Greek text and facing English translation.[4] Beware of books that include 'secret' or 'forbidden' chapters of this work. These are modern inventions.

We leave astrology with the observation that astrology is further confirmation of the ancient belief that the future is unchanging. The movement of planets and constellations is not likely to change.

Since these movements influence the people who live below those stars, it follows that their future is not going to change much either, a principle that underlies all forms of ancient divination.

ORACLES

Oracles were the all-purpose consultancies of the ancient world. There were many oracles in the ancient world, each with a particular reputation, be that for accuracy, clarity or type of divination. Oracles were consulted by all levels of society for all sorts of reasons. Want to know if the war your state is planning will change the geopolitical shape of the world for decades to come? Ask the oracle. Want to know what happened to the missing blanket from the second-best bedroom? Likewise, ask the oracle.

King Aegeus of Athens asks the Delphic Oracle whether he will have a son. The reply: 'Do not loosen the wineskin...lest you die of grief'. The child he later conceived while drunk caused him to die from grief.

Sibyl with scroll. The ancients believed women were better seers than men.
Even Tiresias spent some time as a woman, thanks to a curse(?) by Hera.

Wherever they were located, oracles tended to work in the same way. Those seeking the wisdom of the oracle would undergo purification rites (which typically included the cleansing of filthy lucre from the seeker's money-bags). Then the petitioners would be brought to the sacred space to ask their question, usually posed to the god directly, while the reply would come through a human mouthpiece – a sibyl. While those seeking the wisdom of the gods needed to achieve a degree of purification, this was nothing compared to what those delivering that wisdom had to go through. Which is not unexpected, really – if one is going to serve as a deity's glove puppet, then that deity will demand to get into something clean.

For much of the history of antiquity, oracles turned out to be effective sources of advice. This might sound a touch strange to those from a more sceptical era, but the reasons are solidly mundane. Let us consider the example of the most famous oracle of all – the Oracle at Delphi.

Delphi was the 'navel of the world', according to the ancient Greeks. Even the egocentric Romans did not disagree, for to their knowledge the outer limits of the world were approximately the same distance in all directions from Delphi. Therefore, despite the fact that Delphi is in the middle of a rugged mountain range, people from all over the ancient world came to visit. This was especially so because every four years Delphi put on the Pythian Games, an athletic contest that ranked in prestige just below the Olympics.

A native Delphic aristocrat mixed with visitors from all walks of life and every part of the known world. Consequently, he was likely to develop a breadth of knowledge which far surpassed that of his more parochial visitors. It was in the nature of the Greeks to discuss politics, and in a good week a Delphic dinner-party host might hear the same issue discussed from a number of different, but equally well-informed, perspectives.

Greek aristocrats included Greek women, and since it was their sons and daughters who were due to marry, the women of Delphi were almost certainly as socially and politically engaged as their husbands. The Pythia – the priestess of Apollo who delivered the Oracles – was one such woman; her successful job performance relied upon a nuanced knowledge of world affairs. All that such a Pythia needed to make an intuitive leap to an oracular pronouncement was to be relaxed by the right combination of inhibition-releasing

A screen shielded the Pythia at Delphi during consultations,
as shown in this 4th-century vase from Taranto, Italy.

chemicals – though not so relaxed that she could not pull all the
relevant information together at an almost subconscious level. Then
she had only to give her opinion. Since she was an educated Greek,
this opinion was usually delivered in verse, and couched just ambig-
uously enough to give the Oracle a degree of cover should things fail
to go as predicted. It was a tricky job, but the Pythia was not selected
at random – only the most quick-witted, knowledgeable and, above
all, supremely self-confident candidates need apply.

Consider this carefully crafted, ambiguous oracle, given in
response to a man who wanted to know if it was safe for him to go
to war: 'Go return never die in war.'* Did the prophecy say 'Go, return,
never die in war' or 'Go, return never, die in war'? Only after the war
could the correct punctuation be inserted into the prophecy by the
returning warrior, or by his grieving relatives.

* The phrasing is more elegant in the original Greek.

Prophecy by ethylene

To achieve her trance-like state, the Pythia had a bit of help. According to the 1st-century AD biographer Plutarch, this came from 'gases seeping up through fissures deep in the rock', and modern examination of the rocks near the Pythia's chamber has revealed traces of a gas called ethylene. In low concentrations this gas has a mildly anaesthetic effect, creating a dream-like feeling of lucidity.

To see the magical effects of ethylene for yourself, put some bananas into a plastic bag containing barely ripe fruit and witness a dramatic transformation. The bananas naturally emit ethylene, which acts as a plant hormone that speeds ripening in other fruit.

Modern research has discredited the Victorian idea that the Sibyl was stoned on drugs and muttering gibberish that was 'interpreted' by the priest (who lurks in the background of this 19th-century picture).

As this consultation shows, not everyone approached oracles for advice on matters of state. Others, such as our worried warrior, sought guidance on a more personal level. If the petitioner could afford to travel to Delphi and pay the fee for a consultation, he was probably wealthy and well-connected, which, in the small world of ancient Greece, meant that the nature of the problem could already be known to the Pythia. The issue at hand may even have been discussed at length by the petitioner's friends and relatives during a gossipy dinner party. Even if this were not the case, as any modern agony aunt will testify, humans keep getting into the same old messes in the same old ways, and the same old solutions still apply. Each solution has only to be customized slightly for a particular individual.

As a result of all this, even a sceptic with zero belief in the gods might consult the oracle for political or personal guidance. There was simply no better source for intelligent, impartial advice. Consequently, most big decisions were made with help from Delphi, and because

Apollo, god of prophecy, pours a libation. The raven is shown because it is a mantic bird – that is, a bird associated with telling the future.

Delphi therefore knew what everyone was up to, Delphic pronounce-ments remained well-informed and were thus all the more eagerly sought. The Pythia was a self-fulfilling prophet.

For example, King Croesus of Lydia (a then-powerful nation in Asia Minor) once asked the Oracle whether he should attack the Persian empire. He was told that a great empire would fall if he did. The Oracle was correct, though Croesus felt somewhat aggrieved that the Pythia did not mention that the ruined empire would be his own. The Oracle was also consulted by the Athenians as to how they should defend against a Persian invasion, and later by the Spartans as to whether they should attack Athens, and by Brutus when he decided to overthrow the monarchy of early Rome.

The Delphic Oracle suffered a decline in prestige under the Roman Empire, and was last heard from in AD 362, when it answered a query from the Emperor Julian with what was essentially an 'out-of-business' notice:

> Tell the emperor that the Diadalic Hall has fallen
> Phoebus [Apollo] no longer has his chamber.
> Gone is the laurel, and in the wellspring of prophecy
> The speaking water is still.[5]

While Delphi represented the gold standard of oracular advice, there were plenty of others to choose from, with the oldest being that of Zeus at Dodona in northwest Greece. No one is sure when this oracle was founded, but it was probably some time in the 3rd millennium BC. This oracle is of particular interest to the modern magical researcher because it did not require a trained seer to pass on the messages of the god. Instead, in a sacred grove the sound of the wind blowing through leaves of the oaks carried Zeus's messages. Or as Homer better put it, 'They hear / from rustling oaks / the dark decrees / and catch their fates / low-whispered in the breeze.'[6]

Jupiter Dodomeus: 'With the jingle of brass, the whisper
of the oaks and the voice of the dove'.

This oracular site is well known today, and elements such as the
ancient theatre at Dodona have been recently restored. The springs
and oak trees flourish, and visitors seeking divine inspiration can still
rest their backs against a tree trunk and wait for the god to murmur
in their ears. (It is best to do this barefoot, the better to make contact
with the earth. The ancient priests took this so much to heart that
they not only went barefoot, but never washed their feet.)

There is no space here to describe the many other oracles stretching across the ancient world from Egypt to Britain. In any case, most of these have followed Delphi and shut up shop. However, an honourable mention must go to the magician's oracle of choice, the Chthonian Oracle of Zeus Trophonius in Lebadeia in central Greece. In 371 BC it was this oracle that predicted defeat for the Spartans at

---

Questions for Zeus At Dodona

While the oracle at Delphi often dealt with high matters of state, Zeus at Dodona was renowned for helping people with their everyday concerns. Some seeking the oracle wrote their questions on lead strips, three of which (from the 4th, 5th and 6th centuries BC) give a flavour of the concerns of those visiting the oracle.

Should I serve in a land unit [or the navy]?
Will I do well in my profession if I emigrate?
To what gods should I pray that I get useful children from Kretaia [my wife]?

The lead strip on which the pilgrim asks the gods about children is written in Boustrophedon script, left to right, then right to left, and so on 'as the ox ploughs'.

---

the Battle of Leuctra, and the end of their dominion over southern Greece.[7] The seer who inspired the pronouncements was connected with Astarte, the Greek name for the even more ancient goddess Ishtar, who was worshipped in Mesopotamia centuries before civilization developed in Greece. The oracle pronounced its decrees in an underground cave, which could be reached only through a dark and difficult descent. The exact cave where divination happened is now unknown (though the notorious Hellfire Club of 18th-century British 'gentlemen' tried to reproduce it). Visitors to the modern town of Livadeia might direct queries to the ruined temple of Zeus on the hill of Profitis Ilias, as the caves beneath are considered the most probable location for the lost oracle.

PORTENTS, OMENS AND PRODIGIES

One did not always have to travel great distances to sacred sites to interrogate the gods about the future. If the matter was important enough, the gods would let everyone know, through portents, omens and prodigies – though specialist skills were required to recognize and interpret these coded warnings.

Any major event produces a series of consequences that ripple out from the event itself. These consequences are both major and minor. For example, the First World War shaped world politics for the rest of the 20th century, but also produced a generation of children whose parents would not have met but for the war – thus the ripples from this cataclysmic event affected both global and minutely personal matters.

The ancients believed that the ripples from a major event produced consequences not merely *forward*, but also *backwards* in time. Because backward time-travel goes against the grain of nature, the effects produced by these ripples were noticeable because they tended

An ominous bowel movement

In Late Antique Byzantium, Christian belief warred with remnants of the old pagan religion. A local bishop called Dexianos encountered a most unpleasant prodigy at an unfortunate moment. He had arisen in the night to go to the toilet, and as he seated himself, he sensed that he was not alone in the darkness.

> He [Dexianos] became aware that there stood a wild demonic creature before him. It appeared raving mad, for in the complete darkness he could hear it panting, leering, and spluttering obscenities. He was stupefied with dread and drenched in sweat. So violently did he tremble with fright that his head and neck became displaced, and his vertebrae shifted out of position.
> *Miracles of St Thecla 7*

The poor bishop was found in a desperate condition, partly because of his malady and partly because of what the attack portended. Fortunately the blessed St Thecla appeared to Dexianos in a dream, and told him that these ills would be averted when the bishop anointed himself with holy oil. The bishop did as the dream instructed, and all was well.

to be unnatural or bizarre. Because these portents were so distorted, they bore little resemblance to the initiating event, so they only became explicable once the initiating effect had happened. After all, causes are not always immediately obvious from their consequences, whether the consequences happen before the event or afterwards.

Plutarch presents some examples of the strange, precursor events caused by such 'ripples in time' in his discussion of a world-changing event – the assassination of Julius Caesar.

It seems that predestined events are unavoidable, but not unpredictable. Amazing signs and manifestations were reported. Yes, there were lights in the heavens, unexplained things crashing about in the night and birds associated with omens appearing in the forum, but with so great an event, such signs are hardly worth discussing.

More significantly, Strabo the philosopher reports that crowds of men apparently on fire were seen rushing by. [In another case] flames spouted from the hand of a soldier's slave, though when the flame ceased the man appeared uninjured. Furthermore, he says that when Caesar sacrificed [an animal to the gods] no heart was found within the sacrificial beast. This last portent caused great consternation, for in the natural way of things such a creature could not exist.[8]

Modern quantum theory actually supports the idea that precursor portents may be possible. According to this theory, humans live in the past – that is, everything we observe through our senses is slightly out of date. Nerve impulses take a fraction of a second to travel from fingertip to brain. We hear sounds up to a minute late, depending on how far away the event that produced them takes place; and when we look at the stars at night, we are seeing them as they were years, centuries, or even millennia, ago.

What follows is a gross simplification of an issue that quantum physicists say is best explained by mathematics. Quantum theory states that observation can change the eigenstate by collapsing the possibilities of a wave form. But as we have noted, our observations are of the past, and the collapse happens instantaneously (quantum entanglement shows it happens much faster than the speed of light). This means that to be observed, the effect must have happened *before* the observation that caused the effect. In other words, something in the present can be affected by an event in its future. Once this principle is accepted, it is just a matter of scaling it up to get prodigies and omens as the consequences of causes in the future.

Omens and prodigies are both types of portent. Although there is considerable overlap, a good rule of thumb (which the ancients did not always observe) is that omens are unusual events and prodigies are unusual things. By this definition we can categorize the following events in the year 203 BC as recorded by Julius Obsequens.[9] Ravens tearing away the gold leaf on the temples of the Capitol is an omen, because although both birds and gilding are natural, the event itself was ominous. Another omen was mice gnawing at a golden wreath, as happened at Antium. However, a foal born with five feet in Reate was in itself 'unnatural' (for a given definition of 'natural'), and therefore a prodigy, as was the great meteor which lit up the skies in Anagnia.

Another event to which Obsequens refers – a circular object 'shaped like a shield' moving across the sky from east to west – would today be placed in an entirely different category of unexplained phenomena.

Exactly what was portended by these events is difficult to tell. In fact, Obsequens seems to have compiled his list of portents with the intent that they should be collated against historical events. Despite his efforts, the best that was managed was a consensus that some portents, such as comets, were definitely bad. The problem with a more complete set of observations was that humans kept interfering with the outcome. In the cases given above, we are told that expiatory measures were taken by the priests and civil authorities to prevent any ill consequences, and this was largely effective. Taken to the logical extreme, if we accept the ancient view that the future was fixed, then what these omens actually foretold is that successful expiatory measures would be taken. (As is often the case when we look at the future affecting the past, there are times when one needs to break off contemplation of the matter to go and wrap a wet towel around one's head. A wise woman once remarked 'The future's not ours to see'. That goes double for reaching back from the future to change the past.)

HARUSPICY

While some classical forms of divination, such as astrology, have actually gained in popularity in modern times, one that has fallen by the wayside is haruspicy, the ancient art of chopping up animals to see what their liver had to say about the future. (*Haru* is the same root word for 'innards' that has given us the modern word 'hernia'.)

Like astrology, this practice goes back further than Greece and Rome, for the Babylonians were also renowned for their skill at it.

The Liver of Piacenza

One of the best-preserved Etruscan model livers is the so-called 'Liver of Piacenza', now available for consultation in the Municipal Museum of Piacenza in Tuscany.

For divination the liver is marked with sixteen subdivisions. Sixteen is a magical number, being four times four. There is a loose linguistic connection between 'hex', a magic spell, and 'hexadecimal', base sixteen. If we assume that each of these sixteen divisions of the liver represented a corresponding part of the heavens, then each section was marked with its representative deity, just as in astrology Aries is represented by Mars/Ares, Gemini by Mercury/Hermes, Sagittarius by Jupiter/Zeus and so on.

The Roman version of haruspicy came from the Etruscans, an Italian people who were the Romans' go-to folk for matters magical. In fact, we can still see how the Etruscans went about haruspicy, because divination from animal innards was a complex art. As with any complex art, there were models and textbooks to teach students and to serve as references for old hands. As a result, a number of museums hold sculpted liver models, carefully marked to indicate which divine forces had intervened to give the liver the shape it had. Unfortunately, our knowledge of Babylonian and Etruscan religion is too scanty to decipher which deities were referred to in every case. Sometimes the sculptor had to use small, abbreviated text on an artefact which thereafter had to put up with several thousand years of rough handling and wear before reaching us today.

Once a sacrifice had been made, the *haruspex* (specialist priest) would dig around inside the animal for the liver. The position of the

A *haruspex* works on the entrails of a recently deceased sacrificial victim.

liver would be carefully noted in relation to the other body organs as this was also significant (and was a form of divination in itself known as extispicy). Then the size and location of features such as the liver's gall bladder and caudate lobe would be examined, as would the overall size and shape of the organ. Livers doubled inward at the lower end predicted an optimal outcome.

The sacrifice of an animal usually took place for a specific event, often as part of annual celebrations or as one of the opening pre-liminaries to a battle. If the officiating magistrates did not like what they found in the liver of the sacrificial beast, it was usual to keep sacrificing victims until the gods came up with a liver that presented an acceptable outcome. Obviously, the more sheep it took to produce a benign liver, the more depressed everyone became.

> When he [Octavian] offered sacrifice at [the siege of]
> Perusia, he could not get a favourable sign, so he ordered
> more victims to be prepared. Before they arrived, the
> enemy made a sudden sally, and carried off the sacrifice
> and paraphernalia. The experts on hand unanimously
> agreed that those who had taken the entrails took also
> all the danger and disasters which possession of them
> entailed. And so it proved.[10]

Haruspicy is another example of the future influencing the past, since a sheep had to be born and grow with its liver in just the right shape to be significant for the time and circumstances in which the liver's owner was sacrificed.

AUGURY

Today we believe in a holistic world. A butterfly flapping its wings in Brazil can cause a tornado several weeks later in Texas. No one explained the 'butterfly effect' to the ancients, but they wouldn't have needed to. The idea that all things were connected underlay the art of taking the auspices. An event somewhere in the system inevitably caused changes everywhere else. For this reason, the flight of certain birds was connected with the answers sought by the person taking the augury. (Birds, because they were closer to heaven and more susceptible to the will of the gods – but other magical animals mattered too.)

As we have observed, tracing causes from consequences can be impossibly difficult. Therefore, the Romans (who were much more keen on augury than the Greeks) did not even try to figure out how – for example – a flight of crows was going to affect the coming election. They only knew that it did. Thus through careful observation of the type of birds, the height and direction of their flight and the time of day that the flight happened, glimpses could be obtained of what was to come.

The optimistic position of the Stoic philosophers was that if there were gods, they must care for mankind. If they cared for mankind, they would try to help.[11] Auspices were helpful. Omens too were helpful, but usually warned of something bad. Auspices were generally considered good things. This is why today we refer to the possible arrival of bad events as 'ominous' and good things as 'auspicious'.

Generally those people taking the auspices – the augurs – sought a 'yes' or 'no' answer to a specific question. Once the question had been formally posed, and the augur prepared through suitable rites, a place and time were set for the taking of the auspices. The augur would use a wand called a *lituus* to mark out the area of the sky (the *templum*) that would be used. The area on which the augur stood

AVGVSTO XIII M·PLAVTIOSILVAN COS·

V·S·DIIASO·D·LVCILIVSD·SALVIVSLBRINNIVS·ET·PRINCEPS·LEVR·IVSLL·SALVIVS
MAG VICI SANDALIARI

Even emperors do it... Augustus portrayed
with the *lituus* wand of an augur.

was also marked out. (It should be seven by seven paces.) Ideally,
the area for the ceremony should be on a hill, so that the augur had
a good view of the area of observation, though something to block
peripheral vision was useful.

It was important that once the *templum* was delineated, nothing
should disturb the augur until the taking of the auspices was complete.
The augur could be alone, which helped cut down disturbances. In any
case, it is best to do the rite in only male company. The 2nd-century AD
scholar Festus gives as part of the preparatory rite the instruction
'Exesto Virgo, Mulier': 'Virgins and unmarried women begone!'[12]
The good news is that on occasion literary texts have the auspices
taken by women (for example Medea yet again), so there appears
to be no prohibition on the augur herself being female. Anyway, if

Jupiter disapproved of your methods, he would tell you. Thunder was a direct instruction to call the whole thing off. In fact, it was better to also move any other planned enterprises to another day, just in case.

It was a good idea to take the auspices at dawn or sunset, for this optimized the chances of an augury *ex caelo* (from the heavens) as well as from the flight of birds. As well as the direct imperative of thunder, lightning, comets and shooting stars also carried their own messages.

Because the most significant of the auspices was the flight of birds – *auspices alites* – anyone doing the auspices needed some ornithological skill. For example, a raven was a favourable portent if it appeared on the right, but the very similar-looking crow was only good news if it appeared on the left. The most auspicious bird was the eagle, sent directly by Jupiter, though some scholars (including the priestly Plutarch) argue for the vulture. Lower down the scale, most raptors were significant. If no birds appeared, others might be heard. These were *auspices oscines*, and it was important for the augur to note the time when the bird called, and whether it did so to the right or left.

Birds of ill-omen

Blue-grey herons, in fleeing the raging abyss of the ocean,
Utter their warnings, discordant and wild, from tremulous gullets,
Shrilly proclaiming that storms are impending and laden with terrors.

Often at dawn, when Aurora releases the frost in the dew drops,
Does the nightingale pour from its breast predictions of evil;
These does it threaten and hurl from its throat with incessant
   complaining.

Often the dark-hued crow, while restlessly roaming the seashore,
Plunges its crest in the flood, as its neck encounters the billows.[13]

If the birds in the *templum* were observed to be feeding, it should be noted whether they beat their wings, fed greedily, and if any food dropped to the ground. So important was this behaviour that a Roman general would keep a cage or two of sacred chickens with him while on campaign. The sudden alarms of war could make it impractical to wait for the haruspices, but there was always time to grab a quick handful of corn and consult the chickens.

Just before a critical naval battle, the admiral Appius Claudius was told that the sacred chickens would not eat. Angered by the terrible omen, he said 'Then let them drink!' and had the birds thrown overboard. He went on to lose the battle disastrously.

The Romans assigned the task of taking the auspices to senior magistrates, and used them to ask Jupiter about affairs of state (the *auspica publica*). However, while Roman magistrates used their office for these lofty purposes, there seemed nothing to stop an individual from taking a private augury on his own behalf if so inclined. Of course, the results might yet need expert analysis, especially if there was an interruption *ex quadrupedalis* (that is, the augury was disturbed by a four-footed beast). Foxes, wolves, weasels and dogs were quadrupeds of particular note, as these were especially magical beasts (see pp. 127–37).

Today, those who can interpret the auspices are few and far between. Fortunately, valuable information has survived in the ancient texts. Those interested in taking the auspices should refer to Pliny[14] for setting up the *templum* and Festus[15] for observing the signs. Almost the entire first book of the Roman statesman Cicero's *De Divinatione* is also useful, since Cicero himself was a fully qualified augur.

A fitting conclusion to this section is the taking of the auguries that changed the world. Romulus wanted to found the city of Rome on the Palatine, but Remus wanted the new city of Reme to be on the Aventine hill.

Romulus wins the battle of the birds in this
Italian engraving from the Renaissance era.

The two agreed to settle their dispute by means of
auspicious birds. Each took a place on the ground apart
from the other. They say that Remus saw six vultures,
but Romulus saw twelve. Some reports say that Romulus
lied about this, but when Remus came to challenge him,
the twelve did indeed appear.[16]

DREAMS

Dreams are what Cicero calls 'wild magic'. They are spontaneous, appear without preparatory rites and happen to everyone, whether their person or profession is sacred or profane. So anarchic are dreams that there are few rules for their interpretation, and what they portend is often only apparent after the event has occurred. Still, Cicero, among other classical writers, recorded some completely unambiguous cases:

Two friends from Arcadia who were taking a journey together came to Megara, and one traveller put up at an inn and the second went to the home of a friend.

After they had eaten supper and retired, the second traveller, in the dead of the night, dreamed that his companion was imploring him to come to his aid, as the innkeeper was planning to kill him. Greatly frightened at first by the dream he arose, and later, regaining his composure, decided that there was nothing to worry about and went back to bed.

When he had gone to sleep the same person appeared to him and said: 'Since you would not help me when I was alive, I beg that you will not allow my dead body to remain unburied. I have been killed by the innkeeper, who has thrown my body into a cart and covered it with dung. I pray you to be at the city gate in the morning before the cart leaves the town.'

Thoroughly convinced by the second dream he met the cart-driver at the gate in the morning, and, when asked what he had in the cart, the driver fled in terror. The Arcadian then removed his friend's dead body from the cart, made complaint of the crime to the authorities, and the innkeeper was punished.[17]

During the Persian wars, the invading general Mardonius decided to test some of the famed Greek oracles, and sent servants to ask for a prophecy from each.

> The man sent to the Oracle at Amphiaraus had his
> oracle as a vision in his sleep. He dreamed that one of
> the temple servants tried to get rid of him by saying that
> the god was not there. When the servant insisted on
> staying, the attendant in the dream tried to push him out
> physically, and failing that, struck him on the head with
> a large stone.
>   That ties in with future events, for Mardonius was
> brought down not by a king but one of his underlings,
> and he fell because he was struck on the head by a stone,
> just as the Lydian servant had dreamed he had been
> struck.[18]

Ancient literature abounds in dreams laden with prophetic meanings. A common type of dream involved the appearance of a deceased family member bearing a prophetic warning. Being deceased, the relative knows what is to come, and by appearing in a dream is able to influence the living. Such dreams, in which prophecies are delivered in a clear, unambiguous fashion, are termed 'theorematic'.

Even more common are dreams in which the inspiration comes from an unknown source and the situation is presented symbolically. Such allegorical dreams require interpretation. Modern psychologists would not disagree. In fact, the best of the ancient texts we have on dream interpretation, by Artemidorus Daldianus, a 2nd-century AD diviner, offers an opinion well in line with modern thinking:

> It is natural that what we experience should return and
> be presented again to the mind as we sleep. In his dreams

the lover sees himself with his darling, the fearful person encounters that which he fears, and the hungry man dreams of food. A thirsty man dreams of water, and the man who has eaten too much dreams he is vomiting or choking. These examples demonstrate that the underlying experience in no way prophesies the future, but is simply an interpretation of what already is.[19]

However, there are dreams, and then there are visions that come in dreams, and it is the latter that are truly prophetic. Artemidorus goes into detail on dreams of matters sexual and what they presage (for him incestuous dreams are not necessarily Oedipean, for a 'mother' has a host of symbolic meanings). We also discover that snakes symbolize strength and renewal, because snakes are a royal sign, and the snake renews itself by shedding its skin. Partridges symbolize untrustworthy people, and crocodiles represent your subconscious screaming at you to avoid someone at all costs. Cats symbolize male adultery, 'for the cat is a bird-thief, and birds symbolize women'. A dream of losing one's nose might presage death, for skulls are noseless.

However, Artemidorus points out that it is hard to generalize, for each case is specific. He cites seven women who dreamed of giving birth to a snake. In each case, the outcome for the child was very different, for the snake lends itself to manifold interpretations. Thus one child was beheaded, as happens to venomous snakes, while another became a prophet, for the snake is sacred to Apollo, god of prophesy, and so on.

The interesting thing about Artemidorus is his commonsense approach to his subject. 'That the dream should mean the woman's child would be paralysed is natural enough. She was sick when the child was conceived, and remained throughout the pregnancy. It's hardly surprising that the child did not have a healthy nervous system'.[20]

It follows – as Plato reports Socrates as saying – that in order to separate visions of the future from confused mash-ups of the present, a person needs to separate his or her body from everyday experience. The less a person is involved in mundane affairs, and the more pure and spiritual that person has become, the more likely that dreams will be truly prophetic.

> The human soul [anima] comes from a source external
> to the body...that part which is filled with sensation,
> motion and sexual urges is related most closely to the body,
> the other part, the logical, reasoning part is most effective
> when distanced from the body.
>   Because when in sleep the spirit has withdrawn
> contact with the sensual bonds [of the body] then it truly
> remembers the past, understands the present, and foresees
> the future. Then the sleeper's body lies as though dead,
> yet the spirit is vigorous and strong.[21]

For the ancients, life followed a preset course. Prophecy and portents could not change what was to come, though they could be premonitions that you were supposed to act in a certain way. If you did not, this would not change the future, because the future already 'knew' that you would ignore the warning and suffer the consequences. Often all that an individual could do when informed of what was to come was to cheer up, or mentally prepare for the worst. Often it was the very effort to avoid a future event that made it come to pass.

Therefore, an individual had little say in whether life would be felicitous or tragic, nor how much or little happiness, wealth or good fortune lay ahead. This did not excuse a person from striving for these things, since one could always freely choose to be a preordained failure. However, it did mean that people should not be judged by wealth, power or other forms of success. Instead, the true measure of a person was how that person walked the path ordained by fate and coped with whatever life threw at them.

Courage, cheerfulness and determination in hardship, or generosity and humility in prosperity – these were the qualities that the ancients looked for and admired, and they remain worthwhile standards to live up to, even today.

NOTES

Chapter 1

1 PGM (*Papyri Graecae Magicae*) 4, *The Spells of Pitys the Thessalian* 2140–44.
2 *Deuteronomy* 18.11.
3 *The Book of Samuel* 1.28.3.
4 *Cicero Against Vatinus* 14.
5 *The Book of Samuel* 1.28.3.
6 Virgil, *Aeneid* 6,705ff.
7 Book 11 ll. 20–101.
8 *Aethiopica of Heliodorus* 6.14.
9 Lucan, *Pharsalia* 6.700ff. passim.
10 Herodotus, *Histories* 5. 5.92.
11 Cassius Dio, *History* 68.27.
12 Strabo, *Geography* 5.4.
13 Virgil, *Aeneid* 6.127.
14 Pausanias, *Guide to Greece* Laconia, 25.4.
15 Pliny, *Letters* 83.

Chapter 2

1 Pliny, *Natural History* 28.4.
2 Ovid, *Fasti* 2.572.
3 PGM 4.2967–3006, following the translation of E. N. O'Neil and the original *Papyri Graecae Magicae*.
4 l. 425.
5 Pliny, *Natural History* 28.77.
6 PGM 615.
7 Pettigrew *et al.*, 'Factors influencing young people's use of alcohol mixed with energy drinks,' *Appetite* 96.
8 Zerjal *et al.*, 'The Genetic Legacy of the Mongols,' *AJHG* 72: 717–21.
9 *Acts* 8.20.
10 *Adversus Nationes* 2.12.
11 *Refuation of all Heresies* 20.
12 Tacitus, *Annals* 12.66.
13 Suetonius, *Nero* 33.
14 Suetonius, *Tiberius* 14.

15 *The hermetic and alchemical writings of Aureolus Philippus Theophrastus Bombast, of Hohenheim, called Paracelsus the Great* 193.
16 *History* 4.45.
17 Summarized in Photius, *Myriobiblon* 190.
18 Ovid, *Heroides* 6.8ff.

Chapter 3

1 *SM* 47.19–27. Discussed in Farone, *Ancient Greek Love Magic* 42.
2 Plutarch, *Moralia* 256c.
3 Antiphon, *Against the Stepmother for Poisoning* 1.19.
4 Horace, *Epodes* 5.
5 Pliny, *Natural History* 20.56.
6 Ovid, *Ars Amatoria* 2.12.
7 Dioscorides, *De Materia Medica*.
8 *Satyricon* 137ff.
9 *Love magic and purification in Sophron*, PSI 1214a, and Theocritus, *Pharmakeutria* 1, *Idylls*, 2. 10ff.
10 Juvenal, *Satires* 6 6.15ff.
11 Plutarch, *Moralia* 139a.
12 Horace, *Epodes* 5.
13 Martial, *Epigrams* 62.
14 PGM 4, 355–82.
15 PGM 101.1ff.
16 Lucian, *Philopseudes* 14–15.
17 *Zeitschrift für Papyrologie und Epigraphik* 196: 159–74.
18 Hesiod, *Theogony* 424–27.
19 Ovid, *Metamorphoses* 7.168–71.
20 Hesiod, *The Shield of Heracles* 250ff.
21 Apollonius, *The Argonautica* 1,655ff.
22 CIL 8.19525.

23 Sethian Hoard 16, Wunsch 1898 *Sethianische Verfluchungstafeln Aus Rom.*

Chapter 4

1 Philostratus, *The Life of Apollonius of Tyana* 4.25 passim.
2 Pliny, *Natural History* 28.2.
3 Celsus 3.23.
4 *Uttuku Lemnutu* tablet 3.
5 *The Art of Poetry* 1.340.
6 Hippolytus, *Refutation of All Heresies* 4.35.
7 Ovid, *Fasti* 6.130ff.
8 St Augustine, *City of God* 9.11.
9 Virgil, *Eclogues* 8.
10 Ovid, *Metamorphoses* 1.200–240.
11 *Libri Medicinales* 6.11.
12 Herodotus, *Histories* 4.105.
13 Plutarch, *The Life of Caesar* 61.
14 Pliny, *Natural History* 8.82.
15 22.57.4.
16 Petronius, *Satyricon* 61ff.
17 A. Salayová, 'Animals as Magical Ingredients in Greek Magical Papyri: Preliminary Statistical Analysis of Animal Species,' *Graeco-Latina Brunensia* 22 (2017).
18 PGM 12.401 passim.
19 Aelian, *On Animals* 15.11.
20 Apuleius, *The Golden Ass* 2.24.
21 Plutarch, *The Life of Tiberius Gracchus* 1.2ff.
22 Aelian, *On Animals* 1.51.
23 Pliny, *Natural History* 8.78.
24 William Shakespeare, *Macbeth* 4.1.
25 Aelian, *On Animals* 4.27.
26 *The Life of Apollonius of Tyana* 3.48.
27 P. Godefroit, 'A Jurassic ornithischian dinosaur from Siberia with both feathers and scales,' *Science* 345 (2014).
28 Herodotus, *Histories* 2.75 and 2.76.

29 *Fabulae* 14.
30 Homer, *The Odyssey* 20.61.
31 *Argonautica* 2.179.
32 Homer, *The Odyssey* 12.49.
33 Ovid, *Metamorphoses* 7.
34 Homer, *The Iliad* Book 6.
35 *The Life of Apollonius of Tyana* 3.7.
36 *The Life of Apollonius of Tyana* 3.9.
37 Herodotus, *Histories* 2.1.73.
38 Pliny, *Natural History* 10.2.

Chapter 5

1 PGM 8.579–90.
2 '"Superstition" in the pigeon,' *Journal of Experimental Psychology* 38: 168–72.
3 Ovid, *Fasti* 8 477ff.
4 Apuleius, *On the God of Socrates* 15.
5 *Nero* 34.
6 Josephus, *Antiquities of the Jews* 8.2.5.
7 PGM 13.242.
8 Josephus, *Antiquities of the Jews* 8.42.
9 Translation from Berdoe, *The Healing Art*, University of California History Collection.
10 Plutarch, *Table Talk* 5.7.3ff (*Moralia* 383).
11 Pliny, *Natural History* 28.7.
12 PGM 13 1065–75.
13 Pliny, *Natural History* 18.43.
14 *Lex Cornelia de Sicariis et Veneficis* 81 BC.
15 *Digest* 48.8.2.
16 Kotansky 1994, no. 24.
17 Plutarch, *The Life of Pericles* 38.
18 PGM 4.256.

Chapter 6

1 Cicero, *On Divination* 1.1 (Loeb Classical Library 1923 edn).
2 Soares and Levinson, 'Cheating

Death in Damascus,' *Formal Epistemology Workshop* (2017).

3 Suetonius, *Augustus* 94.

4 Harvard University Press, 1940.

5 From the text of 12th-century historian Kedrenos 532. Bonn edn.

6 Homer, *Iliad* 16.290.

7 Cicero, *On Divination* 1.33.

8 Plutarch, *Caesar* 63.

9 Livy, 30.2.9ff.

10 Suetonius, *Augustus* 96.

11 Cicero, *On the Laws* 2.13.

12 Festus, *On the Meaning of Words* l82M.

13 The Stoic Boethius, quoted in Cicero, *On Divination* 1.8 (Loeb Classical Library 1923 edn).

14 Pliny, *Natural History* 18.77.

15 350ff.

16 Plutarch, *The Life of Romulus* 9.

17 Cicero, *On Divination* 1.27 (Loeb Classical Library 1923 edn).

18 Plutarch, *On the Oracles* 5.

19 Artemidorus, *The Interpretation of Dreams* 1.1.

20 Artemidorus, *The Interpretation of Dreams* 4.73.

21 Plato, *The Republic* 9 570aff.

FURTHER READING

The texts listed below deal with magic in the Greek and Roman world. However, bear in mind that the magical world these books describe cannot be fully understood without a wider understanding of the society that produced it. The student of ancient magic is therefore encouraged to read not only these subject-specific texts, but also as widely as possible on the Greeks and Romans.

Betz, H. D. *The Greek Magical Papyri in Translation, Including the Demotic Spells, Volume 1.* University of Chicago Press: 1986.

Collins, D. *Magic in the Ancient Greek World.* Wiley-Blackwell: 2011.

Faraone, C. A. *Ancient Greek Love Magic.* Harvard University Press: 2001.

Gager, J. G. *Curse Tablets and Binding Spells from the Ancient World.* Oxford University Press: 1999.

Graf, F. *Magic in the Ancient World.* Harvard University Press: 1997.

Johnston, S. I. *Restless Dead: Encounters between the Living and the Dead in Ancient Greece.* University of California Press: 2013.

Luck, G. *Arcana Mundi: Magic and the Occult in the Greek and Roman Worlds: A Collection of Ancient Texts.* Johns Hopkins University Press: 2006.

Ogden, D. *Magic, Witchcraft and Ghosts in the Greek and Roman Worlds: A Sourcebook.* Oxford University Press: 2009.

Skinner, S. *Techniques of Graeco-Egyptian Magic.* Llewellyn: 2014.

Tavenner, E. *Studies in Magic from Latin Literature.* Columbia University Press: 1916. (Note that some ability to read Latin is needed for this text.)

ACKNOWLEDGMENTS

My pursuit of techniques and magical arcana took me down some strange literary rabbit holes, and I am grateful to those members of the academic community who guided me on the journey. Particular thanks are due to Christopher Faraone, for making his work on love magics readily available, and Ann Olga Koloski-Ostrow, without whom I would remain blissfully ignorant of demon-haunted toilets and much else. Thanks also to Jake Fullerton, who sent me the PDF of the original Greek Magical Papyri with which I wrestled for many a long afternoon.

This being a text on practical magic, I felt it incumbent on me to get the feel of the topic by attempting some of the less dangerous and arcane spells, so further thanks are due to the tolerance of my wife and two cats, all of whom clearly felt I was downright deranged.

Above all I am indebted to Paul Chrystal, who originally suggested this topic, and whose scholarly and comprehensive text on the subject I look forward to seeing in print.

SOURCES OF ILLUSTRATIONS

a = above, b = below

Chronicle/Alamy Stock Photo **6, 178**; Falkensteinfoto/Alamy Stock Photo **185**; Sonia Halliday Photo Library/Alamy Stock Photo **158**; Bijzondere Collecties, Universiteit van Amsterdam **81**; Rijksmuseum, Amsterdam **23**; Museo Archeologico Nazionale, Aquileia **41**; Staatliche Museen zu Berlin **140, 171**; Museum of Fine Arts, Boston **65, 79**; Brooklyn Museum of Art **125**; Joachim Camerarius, *Symbolorum et emblematum...*, Leipzig, 1605 **147**; Francesco Campana, *Virgiliana quaestio*, Milan, 1540 **169b**; Christie's, London **121**; The Cleveland Museum of Art **104, 142**; G. Dagli Orti **108**; Detroit Institute of Arts **75**; G. Dagli Orti/DeAgostini/Diomedia **96b**; Universal Images Group/ Diomedia **91**; Gustav Doré, *The Doré Gallery*, London, 1870 **31**; DeAgostini/ Getty Images **153, 174, 188**; Education Images/UIG/Getty Images **176**; Photo 12/UIG/Getty Images **15**; Archaeological Museum of Ioannina **179**; Otto Kaemmel, *Spamers Illustrierte Weltgeschichte*, Leipzig, 1893 **175**; British Museum, London **67, 93, 105, 151, 159**; Los Angeles County Museum of Art **118**; Photo Maarjaara **135**; Galleria Estense, Modena **61**; Antikensammlungen und Glyptothek, München **169a**; Museo Archeologico Nazionale, Napoli **43, 127, 136**; Metropolitan Museum of Art, New York **12, 28, 29, 32, 47, 69, 90, 98, 139, 149, 161, 172, 191**; Musée du Louvre, Paris **40, 74**; Schmuckmuseum, Pforzheim **131a**; Museo Civico, Piacenza **184**; RMN-Grand-Palais (Musée du Louvre)/Hervé Lewandowski **101, 134**; Musei Capitolini, Roma **86**; Photo Scala, Florence/ Fotografica Foglia – courtesy of the Ministero Beni e Att. Culturali e del Turismo **145**; Macquarie University Ancient Cultures Research Centre, Sydney **50**; Museo Archeologico, Taranto **8**; Archaeological Museum, Thessaloniki **73**; Edward Topsell, *The History of Four-footed Beasts and Serpents*, London, 1658 **111**; Museo Gregoriano Etrusco – Musei Vaticani **143**; Wellcome Images **2, 13, 96a, 131b, 132**; Albertina, Wien **19**; Österreichische Nationalbibliothek, Wien **45**; Eduard Winkler, *Sämmtliche Giftgewächse Deutschlands*, Leipzig, 1854 **9**

INDEX